UNDERSTANDING
The Old Testament

John B. Taylor, M.A.

Hosea, Joel, Amos, Obadiah,
Jonah, Micah, Nahum, Habakkuk,
Zephaniah, Haggai, Zechariah,
Malachi

A BIBLE STUDY BOOK

Published in Great Britain by
Scripture Union
47 Marylebone Lane, London W1 6AX

© 1970 Scripture Union
First published 1970

Published in Daily Bible Commentary Vol. 2, 1977
Reprinted 1977
First published in this edition 1978

ISBN 0 85421 638 3

Printed and bound in Great Britain by
McCorquodale (Newton) Ltd, Newton-le-Willows

INTRODUCTION

Since their introduction, Scripture Union Bible Study Books have enjoyed wide popularity both in their original paperback and more recently as the hardback Daily Bible Commentary. The continued demand has led to their production in this new format. They are unique in that they can be used both as a daily Bible reading aid and as a complete commentary on the Old Testament.

A Daily Bible Reading Aid

Each volume is divided into sections of an appropriate length for daily use. Normally each volume provides material for one quarter's use, the exceptions being 1 Kings — Job (six months) Proverbs — Isaiah (six months) and Psalms (four months). Sections have not been dated but where it has been felt appropriate that two be read together in order to complete the book within a quarter they are marked with an asterisk.

A complete commentary of the Old Testament

Every major passage is expounded with devotional warmth, clear explanations and relevance to daily life. Most commentaries follow the rather artificial verse divisions, but here the writers have been commissioned to divide the material according to the best exegetical pattern. They thus follow natural units which allow the comments to follow more closely the flow of the original writers thought.

Writers have generally based their comments on the R.S.V. and readers will probably find this is the most suitable translation to use, although the comments will be found equally helpful with any other version.

	1967	1968	1969	1970	1971
First Quarter	St. Luke	Psalms (four-month course)	St. John	1 and 2 Peter 1, 2 and 3 John Jude Revelation	St. Matthew
Second Quarter	Joshua Judges Ruth 1 & 2 Samuel	St. Mark	Proverbs Ecclesiastes Song of Solomon Isaiah 1–39	Lamentations Ezekiel Daniel	Genesis Exodus
Third Quarter	Acts	1 and 2 Corinthians Galatians (four-month course)	Ephesians Philippians Colossians 1 and 2 Thessalonians	1 and 2 Timothy and Titus Philemon Hebrews James	Romans
Fourth Quarter	1 and 2 Kings 1 and 2 Chronicles	Ezra Nehemiah Esther Job	Isaiah 40–66 Jeremiah	Hosea Joel Amos Obadiah Jonah Micah Nahum Habakkuk Zephaniah Haggai Zechariah Malachi	Leviticus Numbers Deuteronomy

Hosea

INTRODUCTION

Hosea was a Northerner, and he prophesied to Israel shortly after his contemporary, Amos (q.v.). With Isaiah and Micah, these two men make up the quartet of eighth-century prophets who opened up the way for the distinguished line of classical prophets of the succeeding centuries. Of his parentage and family we know only the details given us in ch. 1. Some suppose, on the basis of 7.4–7, that he was a baker by trade, but this is pure conjecture. More than likely he was a professional prophet (which Amos protested that he was not!) and the words in 9.7 may represent a personal attack being made on him by his hostile hearers. He prophesied at the very end of Jeroboam's reign (i.e. before 746 B.C.) and may have continued until about 725 B.C., by which time Hezekiah was already co-regent with Ahaz, but it is unlikely that any of his oracles were uttered after the fall of Samaria and the overthrow of the kingdom of Israel in 722 B.C.

Hosea's uniqueness as a prophet lies in the fact that he learnt his message out of his own personal sufferings. His experience of his wife's unfaithfulness to him and his earnest attempts to woo her back were made by God the means whereby he learnt that Israel's unfaithfulness was being met by just such a love from the God whose covenant she had so flagrantly betrayed. So his message was concerned with the constancy of God's love (Heb. *ḥesed*) and the persistent unfaithfulness of Israel. These two themes, with suitable variations, run right throughout his book. They are crystallized in the requirements of 6.4–6.

Hosea 1.1—2.1   Hosea's Marriage and Family

The problem of Hosea's marriage is an acute one, and centres initially on the description of Gomer as a 'wife of harlotry' and her children as 'children of harlotry' (2). Three possible explanations are offered: (*i*) Hosea was told by the Lord to go and marry Gomer, who was already known as a prostitute; (*ii*) Gomer was pure when Hosea married her, but she subsequently became unfaithful, and so the description of her in v. 2 is a 'proleptic' idiom, implying that unknown to Hosea she had the potential for harlotry within her; (*iii*) the whole story is an allegory of Israel's unfaithfulness to God and is not to be taken literally. Of these, the first is beset with ethical problems and, even if these could be overcome, it does not provide an accurate analogy with Israel as being originally betrothed to the Lord in purity at Sinai. The last founders because it takes away from the book the very ground on which it is built: Hosea's agony of rejected love becomes simply another aspect of his message and is no longer the personal element out of which the message grew. Moreover, if this were allegory, we would expect the name 'Gomer' to conceal some allegorical meaning, as is usual in such cases. The second explanation is therefore to be preferred, and ch. 1 tells us of a faithful marriage relationship throughout. Some scholars would see the break-up of the marriage after the birth of Jezreel, noticing that the two other children are not born 'to him' (6,8), but this is probably reading too much into the text.

The names of the children speak of judgement—'Jezreel' (4,5), indicating that the bloodbath which brought Jehu's house to power (2 Kings 10.11) would mark its overthrow; 'Not pitied', speaking of the end of God's mercy to Israel; and 'Not my people', representing the final breakdown of the covenant relationship between the Lord and His people. The finality of these messages of doom is tempered, however, by a prospect of mercy for Judah (7) and by a restoration of the united kingdoms, when the covenant mercies would be renewed and Jezreel would become a name to glory in (1.10–2.1).

Hosea 2.2-15 — Israel's Unfaithfulness

In the opening verses of this poem there appears to be some deliberate ambiguity as to who is speaking and who are being addressed. At first Hosea seems to be exhorting his children to plead with their mother to give up her harlotries (2) and to return to him, but by v. 8 it is clear that Yahweh is making the plea and is urging the faithful ones among the nation to persuade their mother Israel to return to her former love and loyalty. Certainly the chapter presupposes that Gomer has already sunk deep into adultery, and it oscillates between her husband's longing to have her back and Yahweh's similar longings for Israel (14 f.). This attitude is not the only emotion shown, however, and the speaker (whether Hosea or Yahweh) gives vent to his fury at her unfaithfulness and his determination to divorce, disgrace and punish her (3–6, 9–13). These verses may reflect the ancient custom of stripping the adultress before sending her away (3,10), and may even suggest that Gomer had adopted the prostitute's typical adornments (2b). Hosea vows that he will prevent her from following her evil ways (6), but this only drives her further away after her lovers. Ironically, it is only when she is frustrated in her search for them that she considers returning to her husband (7), and even then her motives have a strong element of selfishness in them, not unlike the returning Prodigal Son (Luke 15.17). Frustration with the sinful pleasures of this life is still the first step which leads many back to God in repentance, and God is gracious enough to receive them on those terms.

Israel's lovers were the Baals, the fertility gods of Canaan, who were thought to be responsible for the agricultural bounties of the land. Little did Israel realize that Yahweh was the Lord of nature (8), and He would prove this to her by withdrawing His blessings (9,12) and causing the joyful feast days to come to an end (11). Then when she had learnt her lesson, He would woo her back to her first love as in the idyllic days of the Exodus before ever she set foot in the land of Canaan (14,15). But this time He will make the entrance-way, the valley of Achor where Achan sinned (Josh. 7.26), into a door of hope. For those who fail and are unfaithful to the Lord, there is a way back and the chance of a new beginning.

Hosea 2.16-23   Restoration and Renewal

It is clear that before Hosea's time the names Yahweh and Baal were sometimes used interchangeably, for the Hebrew word Baal, as well as being the proper name for the Canaanite god of fertility, was also an everyday word meaning 'husband, lord, master'. But if, in Hosea's teaching, the relationship between Israel and Yahweh was to be expressed in terms of a marriage-covenant, the use of the term Baal had to be excised from Israel's religious vocabulary for fear of increased misunderstanding. God tells Hosea, therefore, that Israel is to use instead the term *Ishi*, 'my man' or 'my husband' (16). As a result of this it became customary for some later scribes to replace the word 'Baal' in a person's name with *bosheth*, Hebrew for 'shame' (cf. Ishbosheth, son of Saul, whose original name is retained in the genealogy of 1 Chron. 8.33).

In the day when Israel returns and the covenant is renewed, it will seem as if the Lord is taking her as His bride all over again. It will be like a new creation (18), and it will last for ever (19). The bride-price will be paid in terms of the five abiding covenant qualities of vs. 19 f. These denote conformity to the pattern of God's will (righteousness), consistency in dealing with other people's needs (justice), loyalty to one's covenant obligations and devotion to one's covenant partner (steadfast love), compassion for man in his weakness and frailty (mercy) and reliability, as the recipient of man's trust (faithfulness). The culminating purpose of all this is that Israel should 'know the Lord' (20) in that intimacy of relationship which the marriage-bond most effectively represents. Once again, 'knowledge' is a covenant term and is frequently used by Hosea of Israel and the Lord (4.1,6; **5.**4; **6.**6; **13.**4,5).

Finally, all nature responds to the love of God as He directs the heavens to water the earth and the earth to fructify the crops (21 f.). Even the dread name of Jezreel turns into a name of promise and its literal meaning of 'God sows' supersedes its horrifying historical associations of judgement. 'Man's repentance in response to God's call can turn the Jezreel of dread into the Jezreel of blessing' (Snaith).

Hosea 3   Israel on Probation

Opinion is divided whether the unnamed woman of this chapter is Gomer or another woman. The key is in the interpretation of the word 'again' in v. 1, which can be understood in three ways. (*i*) 'And the Lord said to me *again*': this merely links ch. 3 with ch. **1**, but it is not favoured by the ancient versions. (*ii*) 'Go *again*, love a woman' (RSV), which allows the possibility that a new command is being given to love someone else after Gomer has been divorced. (*iii*) '*Go on loving* a woman', which clearly refers to the unfaithful Gomer. Apart from linguistic considerations, however, the analogy of Israel's redemption scarcely allows the intrusion of another woman at this stage, and we must try to understand this of Gomer, by now perhaps divorced and certainly another man's mistress or even slave. Hosea bought her back, partly in cash and partly in kind, for the approximate price of a slave (2; cf. Exod. **21.**32). As if to demonstrate his ownership of her, Hosea was to keep her from going astray any more and she was to be deprived of marital relationships, even with Hosea himself (such is the probable meaning of 'so will I also be to you', 3).

The application of this to Israel follows in vs. 1b,4 f. The nation is to undergo a period of deprivation and discipline, without king and prince, and without her objects of religious veneration, both legitimate (sacrifice and ephod) and illegitimate (pillar and teraphim). See the *New Bible Dictionary*, s.v. for a detailed description of these objects. The reference to king and prince reflects Hosea's view that it was the leadership of Israel which had persistently led them astray from the worship of Yahweh, their true King (cf. **5.**1,10; **7.**3–7,16; **8.**4; **9.**15, etc.). Their promised punishment was fulfilled in the overthrow of Samaria in 722 B.C., but Hosea looks forward to a day when Israel will return to the Lord and acknowledge His Davidic king. This may be taken either of a faithful remnant from the north coming to recognize the kings of Judah in Jerusalem (an event of which we have no clear knowledge), or of an eschatological conversion of Israelites to the worship of the Davidic Messiah, Jesus Christ (which the phrase, 'in the latter days', makes a more likely interpretation).

Hosea 4.1-10   Like People, Like Priest

With this section the details of Hosea's marriage become a thing of the past: there are no further references to Gomer or to the children. But the message which his family life conveyed to Hosea lies at the background of everything that now follows, particularly in the description of Israel's sin as spiritual harlotry, though this phrase may have to be interpreted more literally (10). This chapter contains the Lord's accusations against Israel and supplies a reason for their unfaithfulness. It is the priesthood who are corrupt (4) and the people are led astray in consequence (9).

The arraignment of Israel is expressed in forensic terms: the Lord is laying charges in a court of law (1; cf. Isa. 3.13 f.; Jer. 2.9). The accusations are general (absence of the qualities expected of a covenant partner, 1b) and specific (straightforward breaking of the Commandments, 2). But it is no use for people to blame one another. The fault lies with the priests (4), and they are guilty on two counts. (*a*) They have not imparted the knowledge of God to people because they have forgotten His law (6, Heb. *torah*). Coming after v. 2, this must refer primarily to the Decalogue, that basic body of God's requirements without which no message of love and mercy can be appreciated. (*b*) They have been thriving on the religious affluence of their day: the greater the prosperity, the more the sacrifices and the greedier were the priests for their portions (7 f.). Instead of acting as a restraining influence upon the people, they indulged their fancies even to the extent of taking part in the licentious rituals of the Canaanite fertility-cult (10). With leadership at that level, what could be expected of their followers?

Upon all who are called to any form of leadership, but particularly in matters of morality or religion, there is an appallingly heavy burden of responsibility. However limited our own sphere of influence may be, in church, community or home, let us ask ourselves whether we are fulfilling our duties to the best of our ability.

Hosea 4.11-19   The Idolatry of Israel

These verses deal with the consequences to the people of the priests' corruption. Verses 11-14 describe the degeneration of popular religion which has set in. Drink-offerings have been turned into occasions for drunkenness (11). Because there are no reliable prophets to turn to, the people have resorted to rhabdomancy, a superstitious form of seeking guidance through wooden rods (12). They perform sacrifices at all kinds of unauthorized local sites, on hilltops and under trees, in the style of the worship of Baal (13). Their young women take part in fertility rituals, though the blame for this is laid not so much on them as on the men who consort with them (14), on the ground that there would be no harlotry if there were not the men who demanded it. And because of all this, the downfall of the nation is assured (14c). This is a frightening verdict, and many modern readers will recognize among their contemporaries the same pattern of religious breakdown and sexual deviation, leading to the same inevitable doom. A people without 'understanding' (essentially a religious term) is as certainly heading for disaster as a ship without a rudder.

Verses 15-19 are a group of statements expressing the hopelessness of Israel's position. She is like a stubborn heifer, which will not accept discipline and so cannot be trusted to roam in the wild; the lamb, on the contrary, by its very weakness is more inclined to be docile (16). Israel is so attached to her idolatry and all her other sins that she is best abandoned to her fate (17 f.). She will be swept away on the wings of the wind and put to shame at the ineffectiveness of her past religious practices (19). The only plea the prophet makes is that Judah will not go the same way, but will steer clear of those idolatrous shrines (15). Gilgal and Beth-aven (lit. 'house of idolatry', a derisory name for Bethel, 'house of God') were northern sanctuaries mentioned in Amos **4.4**; **5.5**; and swearing by Yahweh suggests a breaking of the third commandment, though others would see in this a reference to the danger of mixing idolatry with even the mention of Yahweh's name (cf. **6.10**). If this is so, it underlines the sheer impossibility of serving both God and Mammon. No amount of rationalization can ever make Christ and Belial work in partnership. Sin, like a dangerous virus, has to be isolated if the body is to be treated successfully.

Hosea 5.1-7   The Lord's Withdrawal

It is possible for men to become so inured to sin that they are incapable of repentance. Their sins act like fetters upon their wills, so that they can scarcely raise the inclination to seek after God. They are, in fact, in bondage; as addicted to sin as the 'mainliner' is to his heroin. In the case of Israel, this is because they have the spirit of harlotry within them (4), so completely dominating their every desire and deed that they can no longer be said to be in control of themselves. The only antidote is to be dominated by the Spirit of Christ, who gives life and liberty to men.

Verse 6 does envisage some seeking the Lord, possibly because they have been made to realize their pride and sinfulness (5). But because of their unenlightened hearts they seek the Lord, offering the very things He does not want (6.6), and they find that He has withdrawn Himself and is not to be found (6). This does not mean that He cannot under any circumstances be found, but Jeremiah's condition must first be fulfilled (Jer. **29.13**; cf. Prov. **2.1–5**; Isa. **55.7**), and they show no signs of that degree of sincerity.

In this wholesale condemnation of Israel, none are excluded: priests, commoners and royalty are told to take heed, for the promised judgement concerns them all (1). The place-names in vs. 1,2 probably refer to sanctuaries where idolatrous practices have been leading the people astray. Shittim may have been the shrine of Baal-peor (Num. **25.1**); Mizpah was in Gilead, east of the Jordan (cf. Judg. **11.11**), and is not to be confused with Samuel's town of the same name much further south; Tabor was a hill in Galilee and a natural site for a Canaanite high-place. They had done their deceitful work. The people were ensnared. They had produced a generation of alien children who did not know the Lord (7a). The judgement, however, would not be long in coming: the next new moon would see destruction arrive (7b).

Question: Are there people today who are incapable of repentance? If so, is the cause to be found in their own hard-heartedness or in God's unwillingness to be sought after?

Hosea 5.8–14   The Alarm is Sounded

The historical setting of these verses is probably the time of the Syro-Ephraimite war, known to us from 2 Kings **16.5–9** and Isa. **7.1–9**. It was a time when the distant pressure of the growing power of Assyria was driving Syria to make a defensive alliance with Israel and to coerce Judah into joining it as well. Despite the threat of invasion, Judah, under Isaiah's influence, refused to get involved. She was attacked, probably on three sides at once, and, this time against Isaiah's advice, appealed to Assyria for help. She thus became more fully involved than ever she had intended and could claim neutrality no more.

Hosea, therefore, was familiar with invading armies and the terrors they aroused. He saw both Ephraim (Israel) and Judah suffering in this way (8 f.), but he looked beyond the actual events to the Lord who was ultimately responsible for them. God's judgement could not be averted by political solutions. Hosea saw that appeals to Assyria would not save Israel, for she had a wound that was too serious to be cured by such means (13). Moral and spiritual sickness needs a moral and spiritual remedy. The maladies within our modern society will similarly not be healed by social and educational reforms, when their origins go much deeper than that. The nation which has neglected God needs to repent and to return to Him, so that He can reform it inwardly. Without that repentance they can expect only what Israel was due to receive: a disaster that was sure (9).

In a strange pair of similes, the Lord represents Himself as being both the enemy within Israel ('like a moth' or 'like dry rot', 12) and the enemy without ('like a lion', 14). All the sufferings of Israel and Judah in this unhappy period of Near Eastern history are thus seen as episodes in the judgement of God. What the historian sees as mere political and military manoeuvres, the prophet sees as the direct activity of the God of history. It would do the Christian good occasionally to read his newspaper through the same prophetic eyes.

Hosea 5.15—6.6   Repentance that is Skin Deep

Despite the strong language of the preceding verses and the apparent finality of God's judgement on Israel, it is clear from 5.15 that this punishment is intended to be corrective. The Lord returns to His seat in heaven and waits to see if His people will repent. They express their repentance in 6.1-3. By introducing these words with the word 'saying', the RSV misleadingly gives the impression that God is putting the statement into Israel's mouth. But in the Hebrew there is a clean break between 5.15 (. . . 'they seek Me') and 6.1 ('Come, let us return . . .'). It is therefore legitimate, and instructive, to compare the quality of repentance that God awaits with the repentance Israel shows.

God requires acknowledgement of guilt and a seeking of His face, but there is little sign of the former in 6.1-3. Cheyne describes it as 'a hasty resolution, from which a full and free confession of sin was fatally absent'. It was a repentance that arose out of distress and not out of a deep sense of the sin which had brought the distress, and as such it lacked genuineness. Many who turn to Christ in times of personal sorrow or trouble show by their lack of perseverance in the faith that theirs was no true repentance in the first place.

This should not inhibit the pastor exhorting people in trouble to turn to Christ for help, but it is only as He becomes to them the Saviour from *sin* that they become members of His Church, the company of the redeemed. Verses 1,2 have an air of optimism and over-confidence about them (they should certainly not be taken as forecasting Christ's resurrection!), but v. 3 shows a true recognition that knowledge of God comes to men gradually and must be persistently sought after by His followers, if blessing is to result.

God sees how transient Israel's love really is, lasting no longer than the morning mist before the rising sun (4), and He adds that this is how it has always been, for they have consistently deserved His punishment (5). But love and knowledge are what He wants, in preference to any number of ritual observances (6). The demand that worship should be the expression of an inward attitude of the heart is no new thing, but as old as the Bible itself.

Hosea 6.7—7.7   A Catalogue of Villainy

(*i*) 6.7–11a. Hosea here lists a number of atrocities that have taken place at individual towns: Adam (7, at the ford on the river Jordan between Gilead and Shechem), Gilead (8, in the hill-country east of the Jordan), Shechem (9, the Israelite centre designated by Moses to be a city of refuge and not of brigandage) and perhaps Bethel, the religious capital, where the most flagrant harlotry is to be found (hinted at in the words 'house of Israel', [Heb. 'Beth Israel'], 10). It seems incredible that these villainies should actually have taken place, especially where priests were involved (9), and some commentators take these statements metaphorically, as spiritual murder and spiritual harlotry. But such was the state of affairs in Israel at the time that a literal interpretation is by no means impossible. Hideous crimes could well have been committed by these profligate priests, for when religion goes to the bad, there is no knowing where it will end up. A final footnote warns Judah that her day of reckoning is also not far away (11a).

(*ii*) 6.11b—7.3. Ephraim's wrongdoings are made worse by the fact that they are committed in defiance of God's attempts to bring her back to Himself, and Hosea reminds the people that God takes note of all their evil deeds. They 'encompass them', like 'a company of witnesses which unite in testifying against them' (Mauchline). Sins do not disappear with the passage of time; they live on to accuse men from the past. Only when there is true repentance and confession can forgiveness and forgottenness be found.

(*iii*) **7.4–7.** Those in Israel who indulge in political intrigue and subversive activity appear to do so with the approval of the king and his nobility (3). But in reality they are like a baker's oven, now blazing angrily, now smouldering quietly until the time is ripe again for action. Then suddenly they will break out and overturn their rulers in a violent coup (7). This was painfully true of Israel's history in the fifteen years after the death of Jeroboam II in 746 B.C. Of the five men who followed him upon the throne, all but one died at the hand of an assassin (see 2 Kings 15.8–31). Small wonder that Hosea had scant regard for Israel's kings.

Hosea 7.8-16 — Half-baked and Senseless

The oven referred to in the metaphors of 7.4–7 was the shallow, saucer-like disc of metal that was inverted over the glowing embers of the fire to become a primitive, but very effective, hot-plate for cooking the flat cakes of bread that were the Israelite's daily diet. Hosea could hardly have chosen a more appropriate metaphor. Now, however, he likens Ephraim to the cake that is cooked on the oven: it is badly mixed and cooked only on one side. It is therefore indigestible and valueless as food. Instead of acting as leaven in the world, Ephraim has become submerged by the world (8). The tragic result is that, even though her strength is being sapped from her continually, she fails to realize it (9). 'One of the paradoxes of our time is that while few ages have borne more tragic evidence of sin, few ages have been less conscious of it' (H. C. Phillips). When people are in a state of such sublime self-confidence, they are impervious to the accusations of their conscience and see no need for repentance or for God (10).

A further token of Ephraim's self-sufficiency is the way in which she practises her foreign diplomacy, playing off the rival powers of Egypt and Assyria against each other. Hosea, however, sees this for what it really is: a senseless opportunism which will soon land her in the hunter's snare, and the hunter is none other than the Lord (12). Israel is therefore doomed to destruction, because they have consistently opposed and frustrated God's wishes for them. His intention, even after their backsliding, was to redeem them (13), but everything that they have done has been against this would-be Redeemer (note the repetition of 'against Me' in vs. 13–15). Not even when they pray are they honest: they speak to God in falsehoods; they cry to Him out of insincere hearts. Their only real concern in prayer is 'for grain and wine' (14).

Much so-called Christian prayer can be faulted on all these counts. It is dishonest: we use language we do not mean; we make conventional protestations of love and loyalty, but in reality they are empty words. It is not from the heart: we fail to let God see right into the depths of our personalities, and so our prayers are 'surface' prayers. It is 'grain-and-wine' prayer: we want our basic necessities, plus a few luxuries as well, but it is always a demand for *things*, and not for *Him*.

Questions for further study and discussion on Hosea chs. 1–7
1. What other Biblical analogies are there which make use of the marriage relationship?
2. What do chs. **1–3** teach us about the quality of love that God offers to His people?
3. In the light of **4.**1–6, what part should the teaching of the Ten Commandments have (*a*) in the Church's life and (*b*) in religious education today?
4. What can be learnt from **5.**15—**6.**6 about the requirements of God in repentance and obedience?
5. What are the good things referred to in chs. **6,7,** which the Lord wants to do for His disobedient people?

Hosea 8   False Kings, Gods, Allies and Altars

The Assyrian army, which was a constant threat to Israel's security and which had to be bought off by Menahem (745–738 B.C.) with a heavy tribute, is here typified by an eagle, or griffon vulture, swooping down upon the land. That an invasion by Tiglath-pileser occurred in Pekah's reign (737–732 B.C.) is attested by the record in 2 Kings **15.**29, which also shows how successful it was. This may well have been the occasion referred to by Hosea in v. 1. He, however, immediately attributes the invasion, not to political motives, but to the punishment of God upon a nation that had broken their covenant with Him. It was now too late to cry out to God for mercy (2), just as it would be too late for some in the final day of judgement (Matt. **7.**22). Israel had made their bed, and now they would have to lie on it (3).

Hosea then enumerates four vanities for which Israel could justly be condemned. (*i*) Her kings were not legitimate (4), a reference either to Israel's breakaway from Judah after Solomon's death or to the chaotic state of kingly government after 746 B.C. (see on **7.**4–7). (*ii*) The bull-cult of Samaria was an insult to God and would be utterly crushed (5 f.). This had been instituted by Jeroboam I at

Bethel and Dan, but its antecedents were traceable back to Aaron's golden calf. It had obvious fertility associations and was one of the forms under which the god El was worshipped by the Canaanites. (*iii*) Their attempts to win allies were futile, and would yield disastrous results or no results at all (7). As a nation they have no standing among their contemporaries (8), and in courting Assyria they had acted like a wild ass that goes its own way (9: Heb. *pere'*, a play on words with Ephraim; cf. Gen. 16.12). (*iv*) Their altars had become occasions for stumbling to them and not places where they could meet with God (13). They revelled in sacrificial banquets, but missed completely their spiritual significance and had no knowledge at all of the written law of God, They had forgotten their Maker. But He would remember their sins and reverse their redemption from Egypt (13).

Question: How does this catalogue of Israel's sins illustrate the truth of Gal. 6.7?

Hosea 9 — Fasting instead of Feasting

The Israelite celebrated three major feasts in the year, all of them connected with agriculture in some way. At Easter time there was Passover, the Feast of Unleavened Bread, when the first-fruits of the ripening ears of barley were offered to the Lord (Lev. 23.10); seven weeks later, at Pentecost, was the Feast of Weeks, the wheat harvest (Exod. 34.22); and at the end of the summer came the Feast of Tabernacles, associated with the gathering in of the grape-harvest. It was probably at this last great festival, when wine flowed like water, that Hosea uttered the words recorded here to the assembled crowds of worshippers. The crops, he said, were going to fail; there would scarcely be enough to provide famine rations for the people; Israel would go into exile and be buried in a foreign land (6).

These words (1–6) were hardly calculated to increase the prophet's popularity, and vs. 7 f. may reflect the reaction of his hearers. They accuse him of being a fool and mad, fit only to be certified (7), but in fact he was the nation's watchman, with a duty to warn them of dangers ahead (8). Such misunderstanding is only to be expected by God's servants, when they speak fearlessly in His name. No one likes to be reminded of the consequences of sin, least of all when he professes not to believe in sin. The fact that so many people today regard God as a dead-letter, morality as a matter of convenience and religion as a quaint but valueless piece of Victoriana, should not deter the Church from issuing stern warnings based on

Biblical standards. Anything less than that is dishonouring to God and doing a grave disservice to our fellow men.

In vs. 10–17 Hosea traces the people's treachery, first to Baal-peor in the wilderness days (10), where Israel turned to immorality with the Moabites (cf. Num. **25**), and then to Gilgal (15), where they had publicly proclaimed Saul as king (1 Sam. **11.**15). The combination of Baal-worship instead of Yahweh's service, and human kings instead of Yahweh as King, had made Ephraim the barren and fruitless nation that she now was. There is another word-play on Ephraim in v. 16 with the word for 'fruit' (Heb. *peri*); cf. also **10.**1,12,13; **14.**2,8.

Hosea 10.1-8   The Fate of King Bull

The opening words of this chapter are a commentary on **8.**11, and explain how it was that Israel developed the penchant for church building projects. It was the result of her affluence, built up through the prosperous days of the Omri dynasty and latterly of Jeroboam II. The figure of Israel as a vine was a time-honoured metaphor (cf. Gen. **49.**22; Isa. **5.**1–7) and carried on the theme of the previous chapter. But the more of her wealth Israel spent on ecclesiastical buildings and fitments, the more guilty she was becoming. Her heart was false and her allegiance was divided between the Lord and Baal (2). In fact she had reached the point where she no longer trusted in the Lord; He was no longer her King. After all, what use were kings except to utter empty words and make meaningless covenants (4)? The only thing that drew forth Israel's loyalty and anxious concern was the bull-image at Bethel. This was in effect Samaria's king (7). But even that would be carried away as tribute for the Assyrian king, and its altars and sanctuaries would be destroyed and overgrown with weeds and thistles (8). Aven is short for Bethaven, the contemptuous name Hosea gives to Bethel (see on **4.**15).

There is a certain irony about the fate of the bull of Bethel. Though some scholars attempt to whitewash Jeroboam's action in installing these images at Bethel and Dan (cf. 1 Kings **12.**28 f.), on the altogether plausible grounds that they were intended not to be images of God, but throne-seats for Yahweh, the invisible God (so Albright, etc.), they nevertheless soon came to be regarded as symbols of the deity and were venerated as idols. They were no doubt magnificent pieces of workmanship, made of wood overlaid with gold, and must naturally have evoked admiration from all who saw them. That one day they would float away like a useless sliver of wood on a swollen river represented the ultimate anti-climax. The idols that we worship, the things to which we give our major concern and on which we lavish the greater part of our care and energies, will also likewise come to an end—on the scrap-heap, in the breaker's yard, or in a wooden casket. The only God worth worshipping, and worthy of all our adoration, is the eternal King of kings and Lord of lords.

Hosea 10.9-15   'Whatever a man sows...'

Hosea is convinced that Israel's sinfulness is no recent phenomenon: it dates back into her early history. So he traces it first to Baal-peor (**9.**10), then to Gilgal (**9.**15) and now to Gibeah (**10.**9). Gibeah was Saul's home town (1 Sam. **10.**26), and this may be yet another reference to the evils of the monarchy; but it was also the setting for the hideous crime of the Benjaminites and their subsequent punishment (Judg. **19** f.), and it is more likely that this was in Hosea's mind as he spoke. Alternatively both incidents are recollected in the phrase 'double iniquity' (10). Israel had not changed inwardly since those faraway days of civil war and inter-tribal massacre that marked the break-up of the Judges' rule, and so the Lord's chastisement was as inevitable as the night which follows the day.

Then, in striking contrast to his simile of **4.**16, Hosea likens Ephraim to a docile heifer which has been trained to perform the congenial task of treading out the grain on the threshing-floor. She has had an easy time of it in the past, but now she is going to be made to work hard at the plough. Israel must buckle to and make costly efforts to prepare herself for seeking the Lord in repentance and for sowing righteously for the future. The way of repentance and the taking of the yoke of Christ upon one's shoulders *is* costly and demands sweat and sacrifice. It is only because He adds His strength to ours that the yoke becomes easy and the burden light. But the disciple who thinks that the Christian life is a life of effortless passivity has deluded himself and is not walking along the narrow way.

Verse 13 shows that Israel was quickly diverted from God's purpose for her. She trusted in armies and chariots (13), and the crop she sowed would be the crop she would reap. As in recent times Salamanu of Moab had invaded Gilead and cruelly destroyed a city there, so all Israel's fortresses would soon be caught up in the tumult of a disastrous war (14). And she had only herself to blame.

Hosea 11 — The Father's Love

This chapter contains some of the tenderest language in the whole of the book, as it describes the Father's love for His wayward child. The tone does not however remain constant, but fluctuates severely from section to section. (*i*) Verses 1–4. Israel was loved (i.e. chosen) in his infancy as a nation in Egypt. He became God's covenant son (cf. 2 Sam. 7.14) and was trained gently and lovingly by his Father. Verse 4 reverts to the picture of Israel as the docile heifer and the Lord as her owner, but the relationship is basically the same. God has done everything for His people, and Israel simply has not acknowledged the fact (cf. Isa. 1.2 f.; Amos 2.9–12).

(*ii*) Verses 5–7. Therefore all tenderness is gone, and judgement will take its place. The yoke which was eased from the heifer to allow her to eat in comfort (4) will now become a fixture upon her neck (7). The bondage from which the children of Israel were originally delivered will become their lot once more, either in Egypt or Assyria (5).

(*iii*) Verses 8,9. Such a prospect revives God's tender-hearted concern. How could He treat Israel in the same way as the cities of the plain, which had been destroyed with Sodom and Gomorrah (Deut. 29.23)? Could the Lord ever apply His 'final solution' to the people that He had reared and redeemed? If we find God's judgement a problem, we may be encouraged from this to realize that it is also a problem with God. The tenderness and compassion of God are for ever tempering His justice and it is only in the cross that 'heaven's love and heaven's justice meet'. Peter attributes the delay in the Second Coming to this very quality in the nature of God (2 Pet. 3.9). The door of God's mercy still stands wide open to all who would return to Him; it has never yet shut . . . but one day it will.

(*iv*) Verses 10–12. Here are two postscripts. The first (10 f.) says that God will finally call His scattered people home. The second (12) is a brief summing-up of the contrast between faithless Ephraim and faithful Judah.

For meditation:
> 'There's a wideness in God's mercy like the
>   wideness of the sea;
> There's a kindness in His justice which is
>   more than liberty.
> For the love of God is broader than the measures
>   of man's mind,
> And the heart of the Eternal is most wonderfully kind.'
>   (F. W. Faber)

Hosea 12   The Indictment of Israel and Judah

There are many difficulties in understanding the sequence of thought in the Hebrew text of this chapter (as so often in Hosea's writings), and many emendations and rearrangements of the material have been suggested. Verse 12, put in brackets by the RSV, would go better with the flashback to Jacob's life in vs. 3 f.; v. 7 seems to be suspended in mid-air; and the reference to Judah (2) seems not to be followed through. The general pattern, however, is recognizable. The Lord has a controversy with His people (2; cf. 4.1), and although the brunt of it is directed against Israel-Ephraim, Judah is probably included because he was one of the patriarch Jacob's sons.

Verses 3–6 use the story of Jacob's life to provide a cautionary tale. They play with the names of Jacob ('supplanter', from a word meaning 'heel') and Israel (Gen. **32**.28), showing that he developed from being a 'heel' to being a 'prince with God', as he returned to Him at Bethel and God spoke with him face to face. Now the nation named after him and identified with him (Heb. has 'with *us*' in v. 4) must take that same road back to God and demonstrate their repentance with practical morality and submissiveness before Him (6).

Verses 7–9 deal with Israel's affluence. The word for 'a trader' (7) is literally 'a Canaanite', for the Canaanites were a nation of merchants. But here it obviously carries the pejorative sense of all that that word conveys in terms of dishonesty, oppression and religious impurity. Israel had entered Canaan, and Canaan's ways had entered Israel. No amount of protestation that it was all the result of honest effort would save her from the judgement of v. 9; as a nation she would revert to the austerities of wilderness days and be deprived of all her urban prosperity.

Finally (10–14), Hosea makes an unusual reference to the place of prophecy in Israel's history. Moses the prophet had been God's agent in redeeming and preserving Israel (13); and other prophets had been the means whereby God's guidance and help had always been available (10). There may even be a sense in which v. 12 was inserted here to show that the prophet, like the patriarch Jacob, was also the shepherd of his people; but it is more likely that this verse should go with vs. 3–6.

Note: V. 11 is singularly unoriginal: '*if* there is iniquity . . .', when Hosea has been saying over and over again that there was! But there is a typical play on words here between Gilead, Gilgal and 'heaps' (Heb. *gallim*). Probably the verse should be written in quotation marks and taken as a sample of the prophetic 'parables'.

Hosea 13   'No God but Me'

Hosea's message would be a black one indeed if this were the final chapter of his book. It gives a prospect of unalleviated doom and destruction. There are the familiar themes of Israel's idolatry, scornfully decried in v. 2; of a judgement upon Israel by the hand of plundering armies (16). God appears in the role of a wild animal (lion, leopard, bear) lying in wait for Israel and pouncing upon them to rend them limb from limb (7 f.); or coming like the hot east wind (the sirocco or 'ḥamsin') and drying up the land and everything green within it (15). In yet other similes (and Hosea's oracles are remarkably rich in these), Israel is likened to the evaporating mist or dew of early morning (cf. 6.4), to the chaff blown away like dust from the threshing-floor, and like smoke as it curls away through a hole in the roof (3). In every case, be it noted, the stress is on that which is transient, unstable and insubstantial.

As the reader by now scarcely needs to be told, all this is due to Israel's rejection of their only God and Saviour (4). Here is a striking dogmatic assertion of monotheism, comparable to that of Isa. 43–45. But it is no merely philosophical concept: it is grounded in history. It was Yahweh alone who delivered Israel from Egypt; it was He alone who preserved the people in the wilderness and made them His people. He had no rivals or competitors. The Baals to whom Israel turned (1) were neither gods nor could they save. There could be for Israel 'no other gods before Me' (Deut. 5.7). But what a nation could believe in adversity she could forget in prosperity (6). Satiety breeds complacency, complacency breeds pride, and pride distracts a people from God. For Ephraim there could be no more mercy (14). The warning of these verses can hardly be repeated too often today, as in Hosea's day.

Hosea 14   A Final Appeal

The finality of the previous chapter, especially the last words of 13.14, compels some interpreters to regard this section as a later addition. But this reversal of mood, where each successive statement of doom is followed by yet another offer of forgiveness if the people repent, is quite typical of Hosea, and it is entirely in keeping with the oscillation of his own emotions in his domestic life with Gomer, on which his teaching is based. Does this mean that God shares this same inconsistency? In a sense, yes. Hosea's language reflects the unresolved tension that exists between the justice of God and the love of God. It is resolved when, in response to God's love and on the basis of Christ's death, the sinner repents and returns to

Him. But as long as he persists in his rejection, the voice of God persists both in reminding him of the demands of His righteousness and in pleading with him to heed the warning and repent. As long as the prophet has breath to speak and the hearer life to respond, this must be the message. When life is ended, the shutters come down and the judgement of God is the only way in which His love can operate. For there is an element of mercy even in God's act of preventing unrepentant man from seeing the full wonder of the love that he has rejected.

Hosea's final appeal is expressed in the form of a liturgy. The words of repentance are offered for Israel to use (2 f.), and the response of the Lord to that repentance is given in vs. 4–7. Israel will flourish, as it was intended she should; she will be fruitulf and prosperous with a fertility that does not come from Baal and that is not expressed in terms of wealth and fortified cities. All this is on offer to Israel, but it is conditional on their genuine response. We know from history that Hosea's words fell on deaf ears. There was no repentance, and judgement came. But in the strange economy of God, Israel has not been cut off for ever (cf. Rom. **11.1** ff.), and many Christians believe that God's purposes of mercy will one day be fulfilled.

Questions for further study and discussion on Hosea chs. 8–14

1. What similes are used in these chapters to describe Israel?
2. Using a concordance, read the O.T. passages which tell of the past history of Gibeah (**9.9**; **10.9**).
3. How many verses in chs. **11–14** illustrate the tenderness of God?
4. Hosea's words are quoted in the N.T. in at least two notable passages, Matt. **2.15** and 1 Cor. **15.55**. Study the way in which Matthew and Paul interpret his sayings.
5. Make your own summary of the message of Hosea and mark out the five or six key verses which you consider to be most significant.

Joel

INTRODUCTION

Nothing is known of Joel except his father's name (1.1). Attempts to date him have varied between the eighth and fourth centuries B.C. and have only shown the impossibility of being dogmatic. While one modern scholar, A. S. Kapelrud, argues that he was a contemporary of Jeremiah (*c.* 600 B.C.) because of the many verbal parallels between them, most commentators feel that he was a post-exilic writer and that he drew upon the language and ideas of predecessors, like Amos, Isaiah, Zephaniah and Ezekiel. Indeed he appears, in 2.32, actually to quote Obad. 17; and if 2.11,31 also reflect Mal. 3.2; 4.5, a date around 400 B.C. would not be out of place. Be that as it may, Joel has a keen interest in the Temple and its rituals, though he does not appear to be a priest, and 'temple-prophet' may not be a bad description of him. His message starts from a contemporary devastating plague of locusts, which he sees as a warning of the coming day of the Lord. This should drive Israel to repentance, and those who do repent will be saved in the judgement and will be recipients of God's Spirit and of the untold blessings of the age to come.

Joel 1 — The Locust Disaster

There is no need to understand this chapter symbolically. Its subject is an actual plague of locusts descending on the holy land and devouring everything they find with their customary ferocity. A similar plague which hit Jerusalem in 1915 caused terrible devastation. Trees were stripped of leaves, bark and sometimes even of small limbs (cf. 7); wine prices doubled (cf. 5); and not a sign of any crops was left to be harvested (cf. 10–12). The *National Geographic Magazine* for that year gives graphic photographs which could well illustrate Joel's vivid pen-picture. The size of a typical locust-swarm runs into millions, if not billions, of insects, and so the damage they cause is not to be wondered at. They have always been desperately feared by dwellers in the Middle East and it is only the use of modern insecticides which has made them less of a menace in more recent times. However, Joel clearly regarded what he was describing as a rarity (cf. 2 f.), and that is perhaps why he saw in it a warning of the coming day of judgement.

One of Joel's chief concerns is that the plague has caused a cessation of offerings to the Lord (9,13,16). This may have been due to the fact that the people were husbanding their meagre resources and were not maintaining their priorities towards God (cf. Neh. 13.10; Mal. 3.8 f.), or it may mean simply that there was nothing available to give to God. However, the people are not taken to task for this, but they are reminded that such a catastrophe is an act of God and should be the occasion for national mourning and repentance, under the leadership of the priests (13). Everyone is to be summoned to prayer and a solemn fast is to be proclaimed by them (14).

Verses 15–18 may be a form of words which the people are intended to use. It is reminiscent of Ezek. 30.2 f.; Zeph. 1.7,14. Like many of Joel's statements it contains word-play ('destruction', *shōd*, 'from the Almighty', *Shaddai*, 15). The chapter ends with the prophet himself joining in the lamentation (19), and even the wild beasts are cast in the role of suppliants before God (20). Compare Rom. **8.**22 f.

Joel 2.1-11   'The Day of the Lord is Coming'

Ever since Amos warned Israel that the day of the Lord would be a day of darkness and not light, because it would include judgement on Israel as well as upon the heathen (Amos **5.**18), this aspect of it had been retained in descriptions like Zeph. **1.**15 and here in Joel **2.**2. From being a day for Israel to look forward to it had become a day for them to fear. Joel, however, does not keep his hearers in a state of trepidation, for repentance is held out to them as the way to avoid the terrors of judgement. As the people repent of their sins, so the Lord repents of the evil that He was due to inflict upon them (**2.**13).

The chapter begins with the warning trumpet-blast being sounded, the normal alarm-signal to an Israelite city. The locust plague was not solely the occasion for this, but it was regarded as a foretaste of the coming of the day of the Lord (1). So the language oscillates between the immediate threat of the locusts and the eschatological prospect of God's judgement. The locusts are described in v. 11 as the Lord's army; they are His host, executing His word; and they bring to the day of judgement the same sense of fearfulness and terror as was felt by Malachi (Mal. **3.**2).

In vs. 3–10 the invading locust army is described attacking the city (of Jerusalem?). This is the second stage of their onslaught; after the destruction of the vegetation and the denuding of the countryside in ch. **1.** They leave in their wake the appearance of 'scorched earth' warfare (3), and they march relentlessly on like a mammoth army of disciplined warriors. Nothing can stand in their way. No weapon is effective against them; no barricade can bar their path. To think that it is possible to avert disaster is as futile as to think that God's judgement can be turned aside by merely human defences. In this way Joel builds up to his climax, that a way of escape does exist and that it is still not too late for the people to do something about it. 'Yet even now return to Me' (12).

For consideration: 'The design of the prophet in these verses is no other than to stir up by fear the minds of the people' (Calvin). *Is this a fair assessment of Joel's aim, and is it legitimate for preachers today to play upon the fears of their hearers?*

Joel 2.12-27 — Repentance and Restoration

Joel's call to repentance (12–14) is one of the finest passages in the prophets. It describes God's character, in language based on Exod. 34.6 (cf. also Jon. 4.2); it stipulates the quality of repentance that God requires (whole-hearted, self-sacrificing, and inward rather than outward in its manifestation); and it holds out the hope not only of mercy but of blessing. Note that the offerings men give to God are gifts *from* God, which the grateful recipient returns to Him as a mark of devotion and thankfulness (14b). This is to be a national occasion, from which no one is exempted (not even newly-weds; contrast Deut. 24.5), and the priests are to lead the people in mourning and intercession from the very steps of the Temple in the inner court (17).

In response to the nation's repentance, the Lord has pity on His people and promises them the produce which the locusts had denied them (19), grain, wine and olive-oil being the basic agricultural products of the land (cf. 24). 'The northerner' is an unusual description of the invading locust army (20), for it is unlikely that the swarm would have approached from that direction. This must probably be taken as an anticipation of the eschatological 'foe from the north' which the locusts were thought to foreshadow. The stench from the locusts' carcasses has been one of the unfortunate aftermaths of other recorded plagues, notably that of 1915.

With the coming of the rains (23) a good crop is assured for the ensuing year, and God promises such abundance as will amply compensate for the losses of earlier years (25). This will not only meet the people's material needs and vindicate them before their heathen neighbours, but it will also give them cause to praise God for His mighty acts and for this further evidence of His uniqueness

(26 f.). The 'never again' of vs. 26,27 is one of the precious promises that God gives to His people. Amos used it twice of judgement (Amos 7.8; 8.2); Joel uses it twice of mercy. It is a phrase that deserves further study and meditation.

Joel 2.28-32 — The Outpouring of the Spirit

It had been Moses' wish that all the Lord's people might be prophets and that they all might have His Spirit upon them (Num. 11.29), but it is left to Joel to predict this as a feature of the last days (cf. v. 28, 'afterward'). It was singularly appropriate that the apostle Peter quoted this passage with reference to the events of Pentecost (Acts 2.16-21), but we are so inclined to read it in the light of Pentecost that we miss some of its important features. Joel is in fact saying four things about the last days: (*i*) The gift of the Spirit will be poured out upon all classes in Israel, irrespective of age, sex and status, and will no longer be the privilege of a chosen few. (*ii*) This gift will be the gift of prophecy, and will give its recipients the prophet's insight into the mind and will of God. (*iii*) The outpouring of the Spirit in this way belongs to the climax of history, the end of the age, as witnessed by the portents of v. 30. (*iv*) Salvation in that day will be for those Israelites who trust in Yahweh, the God of Israel, but human faith is nicely balanced by divine election (cf. the two uses of 'call', 32).

The remarkable feature about Peter's use of this passage is not simply its appropriateness to the Day of Pentecost, when an ill-assorted group of Israelites were given the prophetic gift, but his widening of Joel's promise to include non-Israelites who call upon Israel's God. Peter's 'whosoever' is more extensive than Joel's 'whosoever' (AV, KJV), though it is of course implicit in Joel's expression (cf. Rom. 10.13). This may be taken as yet another instance of the O.T. prophet being inspired to 'speak better than he knew'.

The 'portents' are to be interpreted as the normal accompaniments of war (bloodshed and burning, 30), and as the abnormal features of eclipses and supernatural changes in the heavens (31). Both of these were regarded in the N.T. as harbingers of the end-time (Mark 13.7 f., 24 f.; Rev. 6.12). The darkening of the sun at noon on the day of Christ's crucifixion was such a sign that judgement had come into the world and the age of the Messiah had dawned.

Joel 3 — Judgement on the Nations

The salvation of those who call upon God and are called by Him is matched, in the last days, by the punishment of the heathen. They are dealt with on the basis of their treatment of God's people. They had scattered them (the Babylonian exile); divided up their land (which was *God's* land, 2); sold even children into slavery (for the price of a harlot or a bottle of wine, 3); plundered the Temple treasures; and sold Jews as slaves to Greeks (the Philistines and Phoenicians were notorious slave-traders; cf. Amos **1.**6,9; Ezek. **27.**13). In return for this their descendants would have similar treatment meted out to them (8). This prophecy was fulfilled in 345 B.C. when Artaxerxes III sold the Sidonians into slavery, and in 332 B.C. when Alexander the Great did the same to the people of Tyre and Gaza. Doubtless, Jews were among their purchasers.

In readiness for the day of judgement (the valley of Jehoshaphat is probably a symbolical name, as it means 'Yahweh judges', 2,12), the people are called to arms. The famous prophecy of Isaiah-Micah is parodied and put in reverse (9f.), a clear sign of this being written later than the eighth century, and the nations are called together for the final *dénouement* (12). Here at last is the moment of decision (or 'verdict', 14), when God proclaims His judgement on sinners, and His angel-warriors (11) are commissioned to put in the sickle for the final harvest (cf. Isa. **17.**5; Matt. **13.**39). The 'valley of decision', which is to be identified with the valley of Jehoshaphat, is not so much the place where men decide about God as where God decides about men. The cross was a valley of decision, when God decided *for* men, not against them. The last judgement will pronounce a verdict on the individual in relation to his response to Calvary. To that extent it will reflect the decision man has made.

After the judgement, with its accompanying darkness and cosmic disturbances (15 f.), the centre of God's blessing will be a purified Jerusalem. With evil overthrown, symbolized by Egypt and Edom (19), God's people will enjoy an abundance of good things and the land will be inhabited for ever. Above all, the Lord will be dwelling in their midst (21; cf. Ezek. **48.**35; Rev. **21.**3).

Questions for further study and discussion on Joel
1. With the help of a concordance, study the O.T. teaching on 'the day of the Lord'.

2. Are there any events which should serve as reminders to Christians that the day of Christ's coming is imminent?
3. Has the prophecy of Joel 2.28–32 been completely or only partly fulfilled in the events of Good Friday and Pentecost?
4. What does Joel contribute to the Biblical doctrine of the Holy Spirit?

Amos

INTRODUCTION

Amos shared with Hosea the distinction of beginning the great line of Hebrew prophets whose words were written down for posterity. Both men directed their prophecies to the northern kingdom of Israel but, unlike Hosea, Amos was a southerner from Tekoa in the Judean hills, and he travelled north to Bethel to preach on what was virtually foreign soil. He claims not to have been a professional prophet (7.14), but a layman called by God to address His words to a disobedient people. We are not, however, to think of him as an untutored rustic, for there are many indications that he was much more than that. He was a shepherd (1.1), but the Hebrew word *noqed* can mean a 'sheep-breeder', like Mesha, king of Moab (2 Kings 3.4); the fact that he travelled to Bethel, possibly to market the shearings of his sheep, suggests that he may have been a master-shepherd with others in his employ; he was a man of affairs, who was in touch with recent events among the surrounding nations (1.3—2.3); he had sufficient knowledge of liturgical formulae to be able to produce the poetic oracular structures in which most of his messages were couched. His ministry may be dated around 760–750 B.C. The only fixed point in time which he gives us (1.1, 'before the earthquake') must refer to the exceptionally serious tremor which was remembered hundreds of years later (cf. Zech. 14.5), but its actual date is unfortunately not known.

It is interesting to notice the grounds for Amos' condemnation of the northerners. It was not primarily because their worship was interwoven with Canaanite fertility practices (though Hosea makes it clear that this was so), nor was it because of the calf-images set up by Jeroboam I in Bethel and Dan (though this must certainly have been abhorrent to him), nor was it because the northerners failed to attend at the Jerusalem Temple for the great Israelite festivals. He attacks the northern kingdom for their *social evils*, and he lists oppression, violence, sharp practice, debauchery and bribery among the sins which completely invalidate both the worship of the Israelites and their claim to be the covenant people of God. God's covenant, declares Amos, is not a mark of favouritism but an incentive to responsible moral conduct. The two verses which best sum up his teaching, therefore, are 3.2 and 5.24.

Amos 1.1—2.5   The Crimes of Israel's Neighbours

These seven oracles are a prelude to what is to follow in 2.6–16. Before Amos ventures to utter his scathing attack on Israel, he prepares the way by declaring the sins of Israel's neighbours and pronouncing God's judgement upon them. It is not difficult to imagine Amos in the market-place at Bethel, gathering the crowds with this kind of popular invective, for these countries were all enemies or rivals of Israel. And when he finished up with an attack on the sins of Judah, his homeland, Amos must have captured the hearts of his listeners completely, for there was little love lost between north and south. But Israel's turn was coming, and their condemnation was going to be more severe than anything that had yet been uttered.

The sins of these neighbour States were mainly acts of barbarism, violations not of God's law but of basic humanitarian principles. The Syrians of Damascus had carried out brutal raids on Gilead, probably quite literally mangling the bodies of prisoners under heavily-studded threshing-sledges (the Roman *tribula*, from which we derive the word for 'tribulation'). The Philistines took captive a whole population to sell them into slavery (6). Tyre and Edom both broke faith with nations with whom they had ties by treaty or by kinship (9,11). The Ammonites committed horrible atrocities simply for the sake of territorial aggrandizement (13). The Moabites desecrated the bones of the king of Edom (2.1), an act which in Near Eastern thought meant the elimination of the total personality of a dead victim, making it impossible for him to participate in any life after death. The horror felt at such an act may be judged from the description of a similar occurence in 2 Kings 3.27 (which some regard as having been the basis for Amos' accusation, understanding the words 'his eldest son' as meaning the crown prince of Edom and not of Moab).

For all these atrocities God will punish the nations. Men do not have to know the full revelation of God's law to come under His condemnation: they only have to violate the standards that they in their relatively unenlightened state can yet recognize (cf. Rom. 1.18–20; 2.12). Where, however, revelation has been given, the judgement is related to it and becomes all the more severe. Judah's sin (2.4) was mild in comparison with Edom's, but it was just as much a flouting of God's standards, and so the people merited a similar condemnation. All sin, of whatever sort and by whomever committed, is ultimately sin against God.

Amos 2.6-16   The Sins of Israel

At last the pile-driving blows fall upon the ears of the Israelite listeners, as they are treated to a detailed and extended description of their own inhumanities against their fellows (6–8) as well as of their misuse of God's provision for their spiritual needs (12).

Four situations are described in vs. 6–8: (*i*) innocent men are sold up by harsh money-lenders when their debts are only trifling ('a pair of shoes', 6); (*ii*) poor men, with no influence, are trampled underfoot by well-to-do competitors in rigged legal proceedings (7a); (*iii*) young and old alike make use of temple prostitutes (7b; the word 'same' does not appear in the Hebrew); (*iv*) men attend roisterous sacrificial feasts without any scruples about the way the drink was obtained or about the cloaks they are lying on, which ought to have been returned to their rightful owners before nightfall (8; cf. Exod. 22.26). No one could say that these were gross sins, and certainly not in the same class as the atrocities of the other nations; they could easily be excused with the words that 'everyone does this sort of thing these days'. But God's verdict is expressed firmly at the end of v. 7. If morality means anything at all, it must touch the practical details of the way we live and how we treat our neighbours, especially those less fortunate than ourselves. Failure here makes a scandal of our religious profession.

God then recounts some of His unmerited, and apparently unappreciated, gifts to Israel (9–11). He had dispossessed strong enemies from the land ('Amorite' being an umbrella term for all the pre-Conquest inhabitants of Canaan); He had performed the liberating miracle of the Exodus; He had given Israel spiritual leadership to continue the work done by Moses in speaking God's word and witnessing to His holiness. A theocratic community like Israel needed its prophets and its holy men, but Israel's response was to muffle their words and contaminate their consecration (12). Christian workers can be warned that this is the way the natural man still likes to treat those who are dedicated to God.

The punishment is pronounced in vs. 13–16. As Israel's oppressive rulers trampled on their fellow men, so God will trample down these same men, like the threshing-sledge pressing down upon the floor full of sheaves (cf. 1.3; this is more likely than the 'hay-wagon' figure of most English translations). No one will escape God's judgement, however strong or capable he may be. When God acts, human ability is powerless to frustrate Him.

Amos 3.1-8 — Cause and Effect

The last thing Amos wanted to do was to teach a new religion, and it is quite misleading to regard him as the 'founder of ethical monotheism', as some of the older textbooks used to say. Instead he was for ever calling the people back to the faith of the past and to the covenant which the Lord had made with them in the wilderness at Sinai. This was evident in **2.10** and it recurs in **3.1** f. (see also **5.25**; **9.7,11,15**). The point of Amos' message was that the covenant had been misunderstood by Israel, and that its exclusive demands and ethical implications had been completely neglected by a people who saw in it merely a ground for uncritical self-congratulation. This simply would not do. The election of Israel did not exempt them from punishment; it only deepened their responsibility to live worthily of the Lord of Sinai. A similar danger is faced by Christians who, rightly rejoicing in the assurance of 'once saved, always saved', can be led almost unconsciously into the antinomian way of thinking that personal discipline and practical holiness are somehow less necessary when forgiveness is so freely theirs.

Just as punishment inevitably falls upon the covenant people because of their failure to keep the covenant standards, so Amos goes on to instance a number of other cases of cause and effect (3–6). The effect is seen and heard; the cause can be presumed. For example, travellers journeying together have clearly planned to do so; lions growl only when they have taken prey; snares snap light when a victim steps inside. Verse 6 brings the examples closer to their intended climax: when the trumpeter sounds the alarm in a city, it is because the people fear an attack, and when calamity comes ('evil' is not to be understood in a moral sense), people know that the Lord is behind it.

The application follows (7,8). God never acts (effect) without first giving warning through the prophets (cause). But He *has* spoken; the prophet *must* prophesy; and the judgement will surely fall.

Meditation: The more God has done for me, the more He expects of me.

Amos 3.9-15 — Judgement is Coming

Amos wastes little time in attempting to justify God's intention to punish Israel. To him it is a simple matter of fact: God has spoken, and it will surely happen. But he does give the underlying reason for judgement in v. 10. Israel is both socially corrupt and spiritually ignorant. The former is, of course, the outcome of the latter, and the reason why nations are still plagued with the unhappy manifestations of social evil (crime, perversion, addiction, racialism, and so on) is usually because they have lost their bearings morally and spiritually: 'they do not know how to do right.' A nation's downward spiral begins with its failure to exercise moral discrimination; and the same can be said to apply to the individual member also.

In v. 12 the prophet makes use of his pastoral knowledge. It was an understood thing that the only evidence a shepherd could bring to his master to excuse the loss of a sheep to a wild beast was a few scraps of the torn carcass (cf. Exod. **22.**13). Otherwise there was always the suspicion of a dishonest deal having been done. So Amos declares that when God ravages Israel in judgement there will only be tiny indications left of the luxury that once was hers.

Bethel, too, will suffer the same fate as Samaria, despite its honoured place in patriarchal traditions (Gen. **12.**8; **28.**18 f.; **35.**1). A city cannot live on its past (nor can a church!); it is judged by what it is in the present. Bethel had become a royal sanctuary where the worship of Yahweh, the God of Israel, was contaminated by the presence there of Jeroboam's calf-image (1 Kings **12.**29), and its religious trappings were far removed from the simplicity for which it had once stood.

Its most sacred features would therefore be destroyed by the very God who was allegedly worshipped there. The horns (14) were the four corners of the altar on which the blood of the sacrifices was smeared to make atonement for sin (Lev. **4.**30), but atonement would no longer be made. The fine houses of the nobility would also come to an end (15). Ornate worship and gracious living were no substitutes for basic morality in the eyes of a righteous God.

Amos 4.1-5   The Cocktail Set

There are very few parts of the Bible where women as a class are criticized. Isa. **3.**16–**4.**1 and Ezek. **13.**17–23 are two of the passages which share this distinction with these verses in *Amos*. It was the wives of the rich merchants of Samaria who received the lash of the shepherd's tongue. For it was the unceasing demands that they made upon their husbands that urged them on to more brutal forms of oppression of the poor. All that these women lived for was bigger and better parties, the status symbols of the well-to-do. Amos regarded them with the same suspicious eye that English countryfolk today cast at the cocktail parties of their affluent neighbours. The sin, however, was not in the occasion but in the greed and vanity which caused others to be exploited for mere personal gain. As a punishment these pampered creatures would be dragged out of the city and thrown like so many carcasses upon the city's refuse-heap (3, the meaning of 'Harmon' can only be conjectured).

Such a scathing attack could only come from one who had lived his life out of range of the decadent influence of city life. Caught up in its social whirl, it was all too easy for the people of Samaria to see nothing unusual in their behaviour. But the outsider, reared in the rugged simplicity and equality of the desert, saw this life for what it was. Our effete, western way of life could well be subjected to similar scrutiny by a Christian prophet from a developing country or from behind the Iron Curtain.

Verses 4,5 are a separate oracle and consist of an ironic call to worship on the lines of 'O come, let us *sin* unto the Lord!' This is coupled with 'the caricature of their exaggerated zeal' (G. Adam Smith) in proliferating religious ceremonies and in blazoning abroad the generosity of their freewill offerings. The condemnation of all this is not in the observances themselves but in the motive: for this kind of religion is basically self-centred. It gratifies the feelings of the giver and thinks nothing of the awful majesty of the One who should be worshipped in humble, silent adoration.

Meditation: '*O worship the Lord in the beauty of holiness!*
Bow down before Him, His glory proclaim.'

Questions for further study and discussion on Amos chs. 1–4.5

1. Does the Christian Church need to have its counterpart to the Nazirites of the O.T., to bear witness to a deeper quality of holiness and unworldliness? If so, who should they be?
2. Do you think it is still true that God always warns before He acts in judgement? Has the Christian a ministry to warn as well as to reconcile?
3. Is it possible to be involved in too many 'religious activities', to the detriment of true Christian living? What should be the Christian's balance between his social responsibilities as a Christian and his church life?
4. Amos saw the evidence of true repentance in terms of social justice. How should his teaching be applied by the Christian businessman, the Christian trades unionist, the Christian solicitor?
5. What should be the criterion of our forms of worship: what we find satisfying or what is pleasing to God? What does God require of us?

Amos 4.6-13   'Prepare to Meet your God'

Five occurrences which we would describe as natural disasters are here attributed to God. He sent famine (6), drought (7,8), blight (9), plague (10), and devastation by fire (11), all with the intention of bringing Israel to repentance, but the sad refrain tells of Israel's consistent failure to return to God. The modern mind finds it difficult to share the Old Testament's readiness to see God's hand in such tragic happenings. Today only the insurance companies call them 'acts of God'. But the Hebrew prophet saw past the disaster to the God who controlled the universe, and who was therefore ultimately responsible for everything that happened in it. Disaster did not make him question God's goodness so much as drive him to ask, 'What has He to teach me through this?' We on the other hand concentrate on immediate, rather than ultimate, causes with a view to preventing a repetition of the event. This is a good and proper reaction, but it is not the whole of the matter. Personal tragedy can still be 'God's megaphone' to all who will listen to His voice.

Israel did not listen and did not repent. They had become hardened before a continuous barrage of threats, warnings and misfortunes. But one day God's forbearance would come to an end. The door would be shut. The threat of judgement would be replaced by the fact of judgement. Man would have to face the God described in v. 13, the One who is the Creator of the massive mountain-ranges and the Maker of the fickle wind and who can also see into 'the hidden depths of every heart'. Then excuses would be useless. What defence can a man put up when he knows that his Judge can read every thought that is running through his mind? Part of the horror of the Day of Judgement will be the sheer nakedness of men before their Maker.

For self-examination: Is there any recent happening which God has allowed me to experience and through which He wants to speak to me? Am I prepared to learn and to repent, or do I try to hide my real feelings from Him?

Amos 5.1-15   'Seek Me and Live'

Here is a last-minute call to repentance. It is preceded by two brief laments which suggest that all is over for Israel. The nation has been hurled to the ground and has neither the strength to recover nor an ally to help her up (2). Her armies have been reduced to a tenth of their former size (3). But it is still not too late for Israel to repent and seek the Lord. Three times the people are exhorted to turn to Him (4,6,14). Pilgrimages to holy places will not do any good, however venerable the sanctuaries may be, for they too are going to share in the coming destruction (5). True repentance is a matter not of outward observances but of inward contrition, a personal turning to a personal God. Self-reformation is no substitute for it, but that does not mean that a man's way of life is not to be transformed. Those who seek the Lord must hate evil and do good (14,15), performing deeds worthy of their repentance (Acts 26.20). Notice the sins with which Amos charges his hearers (7,10–12): they are mainly to do with social injustice, and 'the gate' is mentioned three times (10,12,15). This was the Israelite's equivalent of the Greek market-place. It was the open space, usually just outside the city gates, where business was transacted and justice dispensed by the elders. If this became the place where innocent men were oppressed and poor people were cheated of their rights, then no amount of religious profession would be acceptable to God. Repentance had to be accompanied by righteous conduct, or it was not genuine repentance.

Verses 8,9 are a doxology in praise of the God who controls the constellations above, and who orders the succession of night and day, and the ebb and flow of the tide. Verse 9 almost certainly conceals the names of three further constellations, Taurus (the Bull), Capricornus (the Goat) and Vindemiator (the Grape-gatherer), but these were not recognized by the Massoretes who inserted the vowel-points, and so we have to translate them by 'destruction', 'the strong' and 'the fortress'. The point to note is that the God who demands righteousness from His creatures is a God of perfect order and control within His universe.

Amos 5.16-27   The Day of the Lord

We cannot be sure how the concept of the day of the Lord came into being for Israel, but we do know that it represented the beginning of the millennium, the day when righteousness would triumph and God's covenant promises would become a reality. Israel expected that they would be vindicated and their enemies would be judged. It was to be a day of ultimate redemption, a day to be looked forward to by God's people and to be dreaded by His foes. Amos reversed all this. Righteousness would prevail, but it was to be ethical righteousness; and Israel fell far short of this. So Israel would be condemned on that day, and there would be no way of escaping God's final judgement (19f.). It would be a black day for Israel.

To underline his point that judgement is ethical and not religious

Amos goes on to speak disparagingly of all the rites and ceremonies of Israel's religious life (21–23). What God wanted was a spate of justice and righteousness in the land (24). Does this mean that Amos was against the sacrificial system? Was this a case of the prophet totally rejecting established priestly religion as being alien to God's will? Verse 25, with its implication that sacrifice was unknown in the wilderness days, would suggest that this was so. But further consideration points in the opposite direction. Amos must have known that the worship of God was unthinkable without sacrifice and other outward forms. He must have known about the Passover lamb and the altars of the patriarchs; the early traditions of the tent of meeting and its rituals could not have completely passed him by. What he did see, however, was that the *priority* of the Sinai covenant was on obedience to God's laws and not on the carrying out of complicated rituals. Israel, doubtless under Canaanite influence, had developed the latter at the expense of the former, and in so doing had abandoned the basis of their covenant obligations. What Amos saw going on at the shrines of Bethel and Gilgal was a far cry from Sinai religion. There was even a touch of idolatry mixed in with it (26). So God would punish the nation with exile (27), and the day of the Lord would bring them no salvation.

Amos 6.1-7   Beware of Luxury

This passage consists of two more 'woes' against the luxury-loving leaders in Israel. The first (1–3) is addressed to those who by virtue of their nobility dispense justice to the people (1b). They are accused of maintaining an irrational confidence in the security of their cities, whether Jerusalem or Samaria, and Amos has to remind them that other great cities had proved vulnerable, and their self-confidence would be rudely shaken (8,10,14). Gath had fallen to Uzziah in *c*. 760 B.C. (cf. 2 Chron. **26.**6); Calneh and Hamath in the north would soon be toppled by Assyria (cf. Isa. **10.**9). What right had the little pocket-kingdoms of Israel and Judah to expect immunity when eventually God allowed the storm to break upon them? By fancying that the day of crisis was far away their leaders were in fact only hastening it on (3).

The second woe (4–7) describes vividly the plush elegance of the wealthy men of Israel, whose lives were surrounded by comforts and whose main concerns were food and drink, music and cosmetics. None of these was intrinsically wrong. The sin of these men lay in their carelessness of the awful doom that threatened their countrymen (6). When things are going wrong in a community, God does at least expect His people to be concerned, even though they may be unable by themselves to do anything about it. When Jerusalem was on the point of falling, it was this which saved some of her inhabitants from destruction (cf. Ezek. **9.4**). Prosperity can be more dangerous to a nation's morale than poverty. It breeds a selfishness and unconcern for the needs of others that can cripple society.

Are we sufficiently aware of the dangers inherent in our own affluent, western way of life? Are we guilty of relying for our security on anything but the mercy of God?

Amos 6.8-14 — Pride and its Punishment

Hard on the heels of prosperity comes pride, and Israel developed all the unpleasant characteristics of the self-made man. In fact 'the pride of Israel-Jacob' became almost a byword in these days before the country's overthrow (see Hos. **5.5**; **7.10**; **12.8**; as well as Amos **8.7**). It was the attitude of mind which could be traced back to Adam—the attempt to rise above one's station and to think and act like a demi-god. It was the sin of Babel (Gen. **11.4**), and of the king of Babylon mentioned in Isa. **14.13** f. It was to bring about the downfall of the wealthy city of Tyre and the flourishing kingdom of Egypt (Ezek. **28.2** ff.; **29.3,9**). It still fools men and nations, encouraging them with thoughts of grandeur but actually bringing them down into the dust. The hardest thing a man has to learn is the way of humility.

Israel had been encouraged by two minor military sucesses over towns that can hardly be identified today (13), but God was going to bring against them a real foe, the Assyrians, who would crush them from one end of the land to the other (14). The 'entrance of Hamath' appears frequently as a northern frontier area, and is probably the name of a town in Lebanon (Lebo-Hamath); the Arabah is the dried-up watercourse running south from the Dead Sea to the Gulf of Akaba. Israel's topsy-turvy standards and her futile expectations are nothing short of ridiculous, as Amos makes plain in v. 12a. But there will be nothing amusing about their consequences. Under threat of siege the population of whole cities will be wiped out. The picture of the kinsman, acting as undertaker and collecting up dead bodies to take them away for cremation, suggests the horrors of a plague. So dreadful will things be that men will be terrified of even mentioning the Lord's name in case they too are struck down (10). Such is the awful end of those who persistently profane His name. What a strange contrast to the Christian's delight in Him!

Meditation: '*Jesus, the name high over all,*
In hell, or earth, or sky;
Angels and men before it fall,
And devils fear and fly.'

Amos 7.1-9   Three Visions

In the first of these visions Amos is shown a swarm of locusts which are on the point of devouring the whole of the spring crop of grass, i.e. the second crop which grows after the latter rains. This was the main crop as far as the people were concerned, because apparently most of the early crop was commandeered by the king as his royal due. The prospect of such a disastrous and irreparable loss moved the prophet to plead with the Lord for mercy on the grounds of Jacob's (i.e. Israel's) insignificance and inability to stand such devastation. The people showed no sign of repentance but, on the basis of Amos' intercession, the Lord relented and stopped the destruction (translating v. 2 as 'when they were on the point of completely eating the grass . . .'; so too in v. 4). The same thing happened in the second vision, which was 'a judgement by fire', i.e. perhaps a drought which had dried up the subterranean sources of water and was devastating the countryside (4). Once again, Amos knew that if this continued unchecked the result would be disastrous for Israel, which for all its boastings and complacency was nothing more than a petty princedom with very limited powers of endurance.

The third time, however, Amos could not see his way to interceding for Israel and God's final words of judgement were pronounced through the vision of the plumbline, a symbol of righteousness and truth. Significantly it was the nation's religious centres and her royal family which were to bear the brunt of the nation's punishment (9), and this was entirely appropriate. When a people degenerates, the responsibility may usually be laid upon its leaders in Church and State.

The visions raise two problems for the reader: (*i*) Why did Amos not go on interceding for Israel? The question could also be asked of Abraham's intercession for Sodom (Gen. **18**.22-33), and the Bible does not give us the answer. Presumably Amos knew that no amount of warnings would bring Israel to repentance: at some stage there had to be a last chance. (*ii*) How can God be said to 'repent'? The word means basically to change one's attitude so as to do something different. When a man repents of sin, he feels more than sorry; he behaves differently. God also changes His mind to suit new circumstances, and we can be thankful that He does.

Amos 7.10-17 — Prophet versus Priest

This episode describes in classic form the confrontation between divine authority, represented by the prophet, and human authority, in the person of Amaziah, the royal chaplain. Amos appeals to the God who has called him and given him His message; Amaziah hides behind the authority of his king. It is the perennial clash between the charismatic and the ecclesiastic which the Church's history has seen repeated over and over again. The professional does not understand. He regards the prophet's message as being politically dangerous, and misrepresents him to the king ('Amos has *conspired*': but, as one commentator has said: 'His only fellow-conspirator was God'!). He makes a scathing attack on him, accusing him of being deluded ('O visionary'), of being a foreigner ('Judean, go home'), of being a professional ('sing for your supper there') and of trespass ('Bethel is a royal preserve').

Amos's reply is without rancour. He is not a professional nor is he a member of a prophetic guild (a 'son of a prophet', cf. 2 Kings 2.3,5,7,15). His calling was from a secular occupation (unlike Amaziah the priest), where he had cared for animals and tended fig-trees (the Biblical 'sycamore', which is nothing to do with the tree known by that name today). His message was not of his own invention or construction; it had been given him as a word from God. It carried with it all of God's authority, and he *had* to speak it out because of the inner compulsion he felt (cf. Jeremiah's experience, Jer. 20.9). It was as wrong for him to try to keep silence as it was for anyone like Amaziah to try to silence him (16). Therefore another prophecy, addressed personally but not vindictively to Amaziah, makes it clear that in the coming invasion and overthrow of Israel the priest of Bethel will be able to claim no exemption. His family and property will be treated in the way all conquered peoples must have come to expect, and he himself would die in exile (17). There is more than a hint here that the prophet's calling was not a highly respected one in Israel. Some may have been in it for the money. But the genuine prophet had a profound sense of his holy calling and a fearlessness in proclaiming God's word which set him apart from all lesser men.

Amos 8.1-8 — 'The End has Come'

After the interlude of Amaziah's encounter with Amos we have a fourth vision, at the heart of which is a play on words (explained in the RSV margin). This is coupled with a repetition of the phrase in 7.8, 'I will never again pass by them'. The artistry and balance of these four visions is worth noting. The first two are of potential disaster-situations, and in response to Amos' plea the Lord repents with the repeated words 'It shall not be' (7.3,6). The second two visions are of apparently innocuous objects, but they both carry a powerful message on the finality of judgement. This is of course expressed in the words spoken, especially in the 'never again' of God's speech, but it may also be concealed in the things seen. *If* the wall of 7.7 was a bowed and sagging wall, Amos would have seen all too clearly the discrepancy between God's standard of uprightness (the plumbline) and the building which should have conformed to it (Israel). Similarly, what are called 'summer fruit' may have been the 'end-of-season' produce whose edible life was strictly limited, and so they naturally suggested speedy deterioration. The horror of the end-time is graphically intensified if we follow G. A. Smith in translating v. 3b as four exclamations: 'Many corpses! Everywhere! Cast them forth! Be silent!'

Verse 4 introduces a further list of sins (4–6) and their condemnation (7,8). Again, not all the sins are serious crimes, e.g. impatience to get on with business after a festival (5); but they are mixed with shady practices involving buying and selling and not giving good value. The merchant was the sole controller both of the scales and containers in which his goods were sold, and of the weights with which the customer weighed out his silver in payment. So an undersized container (ephah, 5) or a heavy shekel weight could bring the merchant double gain in one transaction. It is interesting that of all the weights discovered by archaeologists from O.T. 'digs', no two have tallied exactly. An honest merchant who gave good measure was a rare find (cf. Luke 6.38), and corruption in this realm was all too frequent (cf. Deut. 25.13–15; Prov. 11.1; 20.10). Those who suffered were always the poor and needy, and God was particularly concerned for the under-privileged. So the judgement would fall and it would come like an earthquake and the mighty inundation of the Nile (8). No sin is too 'petty' to pass God's notice.

Amos 8.9-14   The Famine of God's Word

Astronomers tell us that there was a total eclipse of the sun, centred on Asia Minor, in June 763 B.C. Amos would certainly have experienced this and he probably draws on it for his imagery of the last days of God's judgement on Israel (9). In these verses there is unrelieved disaster: Amos can see not the slightest hope for Israel. The day of the Lord will be a bitter day when everyone who is left will have someone to mourn for (10). But the crowning tragedy will be the famine of the word of God. Men who in prosperity neglect, ignore and even deride God's spokesmen will in days of suffering be searching frantically for someone to speak to them in His name. Though we think primarily in terms of God's written word, in Amos' day the word of the Lord was essentially a living message spoken through His servants, the prophets. When there were few original prophets, as against the many professionals who mouthed empty words or quoted second-hand oracles, true religion was at a premium, as had been the case in Samuel's day (1 Sam. 3.1). The very scarcity of a commodity often draws attention to its usefulness, and in days when churches are closed and Bibles confiscated there seems often to be a greater interest in the gospel.

The verb used in v. 12a means to stagger, like a fainting man (cf. 4.8), and men will traverse the whole land from south to west (Dead Sea to Mediterranean), as well as from north to east in a vain search for God. Their youthful strength will not supply their needs (13), nor will any profession of loyalty to any number of local deities (14). The goddess Ashimah was worshipped by the men of Hamath (2 Kings 17.30), and was associated with the worship of Yahweh at the Jewish colony of Elephantine in Upper Egypt many years later. The Elephantine papyri (dateable in the fifth and fourth centuries B.C.) name her as Asham-Bethel, and this affords further evidence of the way in which individual gods were attached to important cult-centres. The word 'way' probably also conceals the name of a deity associated with Beersheba. But like Dagon (1 Sam. 5.3 f.), they have power neither to rise up themselves nor to raise up their followers. *Pray* today for those who suffer from a scarcity of God's word, and for all who try to supply them with copies of the Scriptures.

Amos 9.1-10   The Impossibility of Escape

In his fifth vision Amos sees the Lord, presumably standing in the sanctuary at Bethel, pronouncing judgement upon it and upon all who worship in it. There will be not one person who will be able to escape (cf. 2.14 f.), unless it be specifically within God's purpose (8c). Wherever men try to hide, they will be searched out and taken by God's hand; not even the underworld (Sheol) will be able to conceal them. The only places that God does not actually go are the depths of the sea (3b) and into foreign lands (4). Too much must not be made of this point, but these do represent areas where God's influence was felt by many Israelites to be limited. The deep was where the mythological monster of Canaanite and Babylonian creation myths had its habitation, the epitome of evil, the serpent Leviathan (cf. Isa. 27.1); but even this acted as the instrument of God. Similarly, in heathen lands where it was thought God could neither bless nor punish, exiled Israelites were to find that their captor's swords were still the instruments of His will. For the Lord is the God of the whole earth, the Creator God for whom the earth and the sky, the sea and the dry land, are the sphere of His dominion (5,6).

Verses 7,8 go on to assert that all nations are under God's control, and that Israel's exodus from Egypt was not the only tribal migration that was His responsibility. The Philistines moving from Crete (Caphtor) and the Syrians from Kir (east of Damascus: cf. 1.5) were just as much acting under the motivation of the Lord. This is a rhetorical statement and must not be taken too literally, because the covenant of Sinai set Israel apart from all other nations (3.2), but it is a valuable cautionary word to Israel to prevent them thinking that they are the only people God has an interest in. By their failure to live by the covenant they have reduced themselves to the level of other nations. They are a sinful kingdom (8), and this fact empties the Exodus of all supernatural meaning.

The closing verses present a problem and many scholars regard vs. 8c,9 as the words of a later writer. But it is not unusual in the prophets for a statement of universal judgement to be finally tempered with a glimmer of mercy, and 5.15 has at least held out the possibility of restoration for Israel. Nor are commentators agreed whether v. 9 is a threat in keeping with v. 10 (no one will escape), or a promise linked to 8c (no one will be lost). Probably it is best to take it that in the shake-up of Israel's judgement, every sinner would perish (10) but all the faithful would be preserved.

Amos 9.11-15   Blessings to Come

These verses are commonly denied to Amos on the grounds that they are a complete contradiction of his earlier message, that they would be meaningless if spoken at Bethel and that they refer mainly to the house of David and so to the southern kingdom of Judah. A post-exilic background is postulated for them, when reconstruction work was in progress and the atmosphere was optimistic. If this view is accepted it must at least be separated from the doctrinaire assumption that all the 'happy endings' of the prophets must be late, for such a view is surely suspect. It ought, too, to be challenged on a number of counts: (*i*) Amos has already shown signs of some degree of optimism for the future (**5.15**; **9.**8c, if original); (*ii*) he has shown that his concern is not restricted to Israel, but takes in Judah also (**1.**2; **2.**4 f.; **6.**1; cf. too refs. to Beersheba, **5.**5; **8.**14), and that he sometimes likes to think of all Israel, i.e. Judah and Israel combined (as in **2.**10 f.; **3.**1 f.); (*iii*) there is no suggestion in the text that all of Amos' prophecies were uttered at Bethel: this could well be 'the prophet's addition as he records his message for posterity' (Ellison).

The language is typically materialistic, in the normal style of such eschatological pronouncements (cf. Isa. **11**; Joel **2.**21–27; **3.**18). The future age of blessing is described in terms of agricultural prosperity, but this is not to be taken literally, as v. 13b indicates. It simply expresses, in as extravagant language as the prophet can muster, a manner of life which is indescribably good. Taken symbolically, this rural setting for the golden age is complemented and not contradicted, by the urban setting of the new Jerusalem in *Ezekiel*. For both prophets, the ultimate future of God's faithful people was beyond man's wildest dreams. What we as Christians enjoy of the blessings of the Messiah are but the foretaste of the joys to come.

Thought: '*Eye hath not seen, nor ear heard, neither have entered into the heart of man, the things which God hath prepared for them that love Him*' (1 Cor. **2.**9).

Questions for further study and discussion on Amos chs. 6–9

1. With **7.**1–6, compare Gen. **18.**22–33: what other Biblical examples are there of God's judgement being averted through one man's prayers?
2. Is it possible to distinguish between true and false prophets today? What can be learnt from **7.**10–17 about the dangers inherent in being an ordained representative of an established church?
3. Notice the repetition of the words 'never' and 'never again' in chs. **7,8** (RSV). Are we to understand from this that there is a limit to the mercy and forbearance of God? Is this a N.T. doctrine?
4. Summarize the teaching of Amos about the nations of the world with special reference to **1.**3–**2.**3; **3.**2; **6.**2,14; **9.**4,7–10,12.
5. What can we learn from Amos about the privileges and responsibilities of being members of God's chosen people?

Obadiah 1-14   The Treachery of the Edomites

This, the shortest book in the O.T., deals not with Israel or Judah, but with their kinsmen, the Edomites, who inhabited the mountainous region south-east of the Dead Sea. This people was descended from Esau, Jacob's twin, and was always felt to have a real kinship with the Israelites, though this showed itself not so much in mutual assistance as in hostile recriminations and charges of treachery (10). Certainly no love was lost between the two nations, and this can be traced back to Moses' day (Num. 20.14-21). There were frequent battles and occasional massacres in the days of the united monarchy, and later, in Amaziah's reign (c. 796-767 B.C.), 20,000 Edomites were slaughtered in one operation (2 Chron. 25.11 f.). So the fault was not all on one side. Edom's crowning perfidy, however, was to take advantage of Judah's downfall in 587 B.C. and to invade her territory while Jerusalem was being sacked.

This latest episode was the occasion for the accusations of vs. 10-14, and accounts for the bitterness of the anti-Edomite oracles in Jer. 49.7-22; Ezek. 25.12-14; 35.15; cf. also Psa. 137.7; Lam. 4.21 f. Because of this Obadiah warns that Edom will shortly fall (1-4), and her destruction will be complete (5-9). In these verses two features are mentioned for which Edom was renowned. (i) Her wisdom would come to an end (8; cf. Jer. 49.7; and there are grounds for thinking that Job originally had an Edomite setting). (ii) Her capital city, Sela (3, RSV margin), the modern Petra, perched high up in the mountains, which was fondly thought to be impregnable, would be brought low.

Subsequent history saw the fulfilment of these predictions. The Edomites were driven out of their territory by the Arabs, their former allies, during the fifth century B.C. and had to take refuge in Southern Judah where eventually they became absorbed into Judaism (7). Ironically, it was an Edomite, Herod the Great, who was Jesus' bitterest foe when He was born in Bethlehem, and another Herod who connived at His death.

Notes: 'Teman' (9) was one of the chief cities of Edom and the home of Eliphaz, one of Job's friends; 'Mount Esau' (8 f.) refers to Mount Seir, a prominent landmark in Edom.

Obadiah 15-21   Edom's Punishment on the Day of the Lord

Edom's sins are to be judged according to the law of retribution when the day of the Lord comes, and this is a concept that appears frequently in the Bible. At the last day, wrongs will be righted and the present imbalance between the state of the wicked and the righteous will be rectified. This is well expressed in the song of Mary (the Magnificat: Luke 1.46–55), which shows that the birth of Jesus was thought to be heralding a new age, the beginning of the last days in fact. The retributive principle in the doctrine of judgement has to be understood as a vindication of God's righteousness, and not as vindictiveness against the sinner—a very definite distinction, which is not always recognized.

Edom's total overthrow is expressed also in terms of draining the cup of God's wrath (16; cf. Jer. 25.15–28); and being burnt up like a field of stubble (18; cf. Mal. 4. 1–3). The only place that will survive is the holy Mount Zion (the very antithesis of Mount Esau), where some will find salvation (17, quoted in Joel 2.32). In contrast with the dispossessed Edomites, this remnant of the house of Jacob will then be able to take possession of all their inheritance, everything that by right belongs to them. This is elaborated in vs. 19 f., where the inhabitants of those parts of Palestine in which encroachments had been made will retake their land and overflow into their enemies' territory. (The Negeb is the southern desert; the Shephelah is the low hill country in West Palestine, bordering on Philistia; Ephraim and Samaria comprise the former northern kingdom of Israel; Gilead is east of Jordan from Benjamin's territory). Furthermore, the exiles from Israel, dispossessed in 722 B.C., will occupy the whole of the south. So the Promised Land will belong to God's people once again, from far north to deep south. (Halah is in Mesopotamia, cf. 2 Kings 17.6; Sepharad is Sardis in Asia Minor, though in modern Hebrew it is wrongly taken as Spain—hence the Sephardic Jews.)

Obadiah's final words (21) show that he sees the day of the Lord not simply as a victory for Israelite nationalism, but as the inauguration of God's kingdom upon earth when all enemies will recognize His authority. The verse unconsciously foreshadows the time when the only Saviour would reign as King in Jerusalem, the city of His crucifixion.

Jonah

INTRODUCTION

We know nothing of Jonah, the son of Amittai, except the passing reference to him in 2 Kings 14.25, which would date him early in the eighth century B.C. The book which bears his name does not profess to be written by him and a number of indications may suggest that it is post-exilic and written about him; e.g. 3.3 may reflect a time when Nineveh was no more (it was destroyed in 612 B.C.). Most of the argument concerning the book has centred on its historicity and the identification of the 'great fish', misleadingly called a whale by some N.T. translators. The result of this has been to divert attention from the message of the book, which is shot through with hidden meaning and nice innuendos. It is possible to interpret the book either as history or as parable without impugning the infallibility of Christ's words (Matt. 12.40; Luke 11.30) and without discarding a high view of Scripture (see *New Bible Dictionary* on 'Jonah, Book of'). If we conclude that the evidence favours the historical interpretation, we nevertheless have to see in the telling of the incident a strong didactic note: it is history with a moral. And the moral is the message that the God of the Hebrews has a concern for the whole world.

Jonah 1.1-10   Running away from God

In his attempt to evade his duty to God and his responsibility to his fellow men, Jonah was being thoroughly human, and so all who read about him see something of themselves in his character. He may also be taken as representing his people, the Jews, who were quite able to produce the correct religious formulae (1.9; 4.2b) but were less willing to fulfil the responsibilities that were theirs under the Abrahamic covenant (cf. Gen. 12.3; 22.18) and to act as a light to the nations (Isa. 42.6). Judaism has always wavered between its concern to maintain its own distinctiveness, with a resultant exclusivism, and its sense of responsibility to the world: it has not often been a missionary force to be reckoned with (see, however, Matt. 23.15). So the message of Jonah is addressed to the Church as well as to the individual.

It is at first strange that Jonah should have wanted to avoid taking the message of judgement to the people of Nineveh. Later events show that what he baulked at was not the message that God would overthrow Nineveh, but the fact that inherent in the preaching of judgement was the possibility of the people's repentance, with the consequence that God would forgive and the preacher would appear discredited (4.2). The story of Jonah, therefore, probes deep into the preacher's motives and has much to say to Christian workers today.

Notice the subtleties in these opening verses: Jonah's impetuous haste to get away from the Lord (mentioned three times, 3,10); the personal cost involved ('he paid the fare', 3); the fact that when all were praying, Jonah was asleep (5); the way in which Jonah's guilt was identified by heathen men using lots, who are consistently shown in a better light than the prophet (5,6,10,14,16); the hollowness of Jonah's profession of faith (9). In contrast with the Ninevites' wickedness and the mariners' superstitions, Jonah is marked down as the one to whom the real guilt attaches, and he is still a long way from recognizing it himself. Yet the prime need for the man who preaches judgement to others is that he should know himself and his own failings first.

Prayer: Psalm 139. 23f.

Jonah 1.11-17   A Living Sacrifice

The sheer goodness and humanity of these heathen sailors, in not blaming Jonah for bringing such trouble upon them and then in trying their hardest to save his life, are a silent condemnation of Jonah's unwillingness to take the word of the Lord to the heathen Ninevites. The consideration they showed is in marked contrast to Jonah's lack of it. He did, however, see that the only way for them to be saved was by offering his own life as a sacrifice to be thrown into the raging waters. There may be a touch of irony here, in that he was prepared to make the grand gesture but not prepared to obey the call of God to less spectacular service. Alternatively, the offer may represent Jonah's first stage in self-knowledge and repentance, though there is not much contrition in his speech of v. 12. However, the result of his sacrifice is that the wind drops and the sailors are converted! Where words fail to convince, sacrificial action succeeds. But even so the reader cannot help wondering, in the light of 4.1, whether Jonah would have been pleased or sorry at this turn of events, had he known about it.

Meanwhile, he was swallowed up by a passing fish (17). All kinds of attempts have been made to defend the credibility, or at least the feasibility, of this episode, but none with any success. We must frankly admit that if the incident is true and the book of Jonah historical, this is miraculous—as unique in its way as the resurrection, with which our Lord compared it (Matt. 12.40). If the book is taken as a parable, of course, the question does not arise. But we do know that sperm whales and large sharks capable of swallowing a man have been identified in the East Mediterranean, and it is probably one of these creatures that is meant by Jonah's 'great fish'.

It is easy to see that Jonah's offer to die for the safety of the sailors would have been loudly applauded by generations of Jewish readers. The same concept underlay Caiaphas's unconscious prophecy of the death of Christ (John 11.49 f.). But for one man to die for others, to be preserved in apparent death and to be brought out alive with a commission to take the word of the Lord to the Gentiles, can be paralleled only in the light of Christ's resurrection, and could not have been thought up by anyone but the One who was to fulfil that same pattern in His own experience. This was 'the sign of the prophet Jonah' which the Jews signally failed to understand.

Jonah 2 — Out of the Depths

The style of this psalm uttered by Jonah from inside the fish is very similar to that of the psalm of deliverance used by Israelites when they escaped from death or recovered from serious illness. Parallels to it may be found in Pss. 18.4–6; 88.1–12; 130.1 f. Although the sentiments expressed can be taken metaphorically, as they sometimes are in similar language in the *Psalms*, they nevertheless have a remarkably literal appropriateness to Jonah's actual situation (e.g. 'out of the belly of Sheol', which means 'at death's door', v. 2; and the engulfing by the waters, which was a Hebrew metaphor for any kind of death, not just drowning, vs. 3,5; cf. Psa. 42.7). The result is that Jonah's words can be taken up by any reader who has gone through deep water (metaphorically!) and found the Lord's deliverance from it. Note, incidentally, that Jonah considers his salvation already to have taken place and that the fish's stomach was actually a place of safety from a watery grave! This does not encourage us to follow those who interpret the book allegorically and who see the great fish as a symbol of the Exile, swallowing up Israel and eventually returning him to his own land: Babylon was hardly a haven from which psalms of thanksgiving could be sung (cf. Psa. 137.1–7).

The psalm well illustrates some basic elements of effective prayer: (*i*) a deep sense of distress in which what is felt most keenly is being far from God's presence (2,4); (*ii*) crying earnestly to God for help (2,4,7); (*iii*) showing one's thankfulness for God's mercy by proclaiming the news to all who will hear, by offering sacrifices to Him and by paying vows (2,9; cf. Psa. 116.12–14); (*iv*) a resultant conviction that neither men nor idols can do what the Lord can do: only He can be relied upon to save (8,9b).

Jonah 3   Nineveh's Repentance

The terms of Jonah's commission are repeated, but this time the demand on his obedience is extended: before he had simply to denounce Nineveh's wickedness (1.2), but now he is to be completely ready for anything that God may want him to say (3.2). The preacher's calling is to be the servant of God's word, not the exponent of the message he himself would like to preach.

The size of Nineveh has been an acute problem for some. Critics have too readily rejected it as exaggeration, comparing the actual dimensions of the ancient city (roughly $1\frac{1}{2}$ miles by 3 miles in extent, according to Felix Jones's survey in the last century) with the Bible's 60–75 miles breadth ('three days' journey', v. 3). The repeated phrase, 'that great city', however, suggests that we are here dealing with the whole of the administrative district of Nineveh, which incorporated the three cities of Hatra, Nimrud and Khorsabad, as well as the capital itself and which covered an area up to 60 miles across. (Compare the confusion which often exists between the City of London and Greater London.)

The result of Jonah's preaching was an immediate repentance which, even though it is not attested (hardly surprisingly) from ancient secular sources, warranted the commendation of Jesus Christ (Matt. **12.41**; Luke **11.32**). We cannot say whether other circumstances combined with Jonah's message to condition his hearers to respond in this way, but if this were so, it would be fully in keeping with the Holy Spirit's way of preparing hearts by all manner of means before bringing the word of God to act like a spark to ignite the kindling. The extent of the repentance is shown by its effect on the king, the people and even the livestock of the area! Once again this is told in order to set Jonah's grudging spirit in contrast with the heathen's full-souled responsiveness. Whereas he as a Jew could be confident of God's mercy, they dare not presume on it and can only repent and plead that God may yet relent (9). God does so, and He shows thereby that He is concerned for all men, and not just for the Jew, and that His judgement can always be averted by sincere repentance. He is not so inflexible that He cannot have mercy on the penitent sinner.

Jonah 4   Lack of Sympathy Rebuked

Now at last Jonah is cast in his very worst light. By his displeasure at God's mercy to Nineveh he shows up the falsity of his motives all along the line. Here is Jonah, the 'narrow little nationalist', disappointed that the heathen are not getting their deserts and yet mouthing the pious formula describing God's generous and forgiving nature (2). The fact is that, although he believes in a God who has these qualities, he wants them to be reserved for Israel alone. But God wants to show His love and mercy to all the world, and offers repentance even to the Gentiles. Judaism found this as difficult to accept as Jonah did, and that is why Jesus occasionally harped on O.T. references like this to the blessing of non-Israelites (cf. also Luke **4**.24–27), but even so the early Church needed some persuading that the gospel was for any but the Jews (cf. Acts **10**.45; **11**.1–18).

Jonah's lesson was a sharp one. When Elijah had felt suicidal, God treated him gently (1 Kings **19**.4–18). Jonah could be shown no such mercy. By a series of miraculous circumstances he was made to grieve deeply over the loss of a plant that had given him shade from the sun's heat ('gourd' was probably the large-leafed castor oil plant). If he was justified in feeling so upset about the loss of an inanimate object to whose existence he had contributed nothing, was not God permitted to show some concern for thousands of Ninevites who, for all their ignorance of His laws (expressed as not knowing their right hand from their left, i.e. without the basics of knowledge), were His creation?

The book ends with the question, leaving the reader to draw his own conclusion. At its simplest it is asking the reader whether he has any feelings of sympathy or humanity for his fellow men and, if so, whether he cannot attribute at least as much to the heart of God. As soon as this is allowed, exclusiveness is broken down and the extent of God's sympathy is seen to be as wide as His world. In a final touch of irony, the writer adds the words 'and also much cattle', as if to say, 'Even if you can countenance the destruction of thousands of people, just think what a terrible waste of livestock would be involved!'

Questions for further study and discussion on Obadiah and Jonah

1. What is the value of including in the Bible a book like *Obadiah*, which deals mainly with non-Israelites?
2. Contrast the treatment meted out to the Edomites (in *Obadiah*) with that of the Ninevites (in *Jonah*). Did the Edomites have opportunity to repent?
3. Which other O.T. books reflect the Jewish sense of mission to the Gentiles, and which reflect their exclusiveness?
4. Are there any signs in Jon. **3** and **4** that Jonah had learnt anything from his earlier experiences? Was he in any sense a changed man?
5. Relate the message of Jonah to Peter's vision in Acts **10**. What similarities can you see?

Micah

INTRODUCTION

Micah was a Judean peasant from Moresheth in the south-west of Palestine, not far from Philistine territory. His prophecies dealt mainly with Jerusalem and were probably uttered there on occasional visits. His vigorous championing of the cause of the under-privileged poor against the oppressive rich indicates that the social sins which Amos saw in Israel were to be found in Judah, too. He was also concerned to attack the religious attitudes of his time and, in particular, the view that God would protect Jerusalem irrespective of the people's conduct. So the religious leaders of the nation were marked out for special condemnation for their failure in leadership (3.1–12).

Micah exercised his ministry during the last third of the eighth century and was remembered in Jeremiah's time for his influence on Hezekiah, probably around the time of Sennacherib's siege of Jerusalem in 701 B.C. (cf. Jer. 26.18 f.). Attempts by critical scholars to deny to his authorship everything but the first three chapters are now losing support, and this minor and little-known prophet is being increasingly recognized as the important figure that he was.

Micah 1   A Sad Tale of Two Cities

While Micah predicts the fall of Samaria in 722 B.C. (6), it is clear from this chapter that he is mainly concerned with Judah and Jerusalem (5b,9,12). One of the important themes of his prophecy is that Jerusalem is in danger of suffering the same fate as Samaria. When the armies of Sennacherib actually moved against the Judean capital to besiege it (read the dramatic story in 2 Kings **18**.13–19, 37), it seemed as if all Micah's predictions were about to be fulfilled. By the miracle of the plague which decimated the Assyrian army, a memorable deliverance came to Jerusalem and Micah's warnings came to nothing. The suggestion made by some scholars that he was thus discredited and compelled to retire from prophetic life is hardly borne out by the reputation he acquired within the next hundred years (cf. Jer. **26**.18 f.).

Verses 2–9 describe the Lord as descending from heaven (2: 'His holy temple' is not an earthly dwelling) and treading upon the mountain-tops, to the accompaniment of earthquakes and volcanic eruption (4). The cause of His wrath is the sin of Israel and Judah, and the prophet predicts that Samaria will become a heap of ruins before Him. All her idolatry is going to be stamped out completely

(7) and she will no longer be a city, only a place for growing vines (6). Micah mourns for her, but his grief is due chiefly to the fact that the disease of Samaria has infected Jerusalem, and so her turn will come next (9).

A sudden change of style follows (10–16) and we are given a graphic description of the approach of an invading army from the Philistine coastal plain, through the Judean foothills (and Micah's home town) and up to Jerusalem. Gath had been destroyed some years before and Micah's opening words were now proverbial for disaster (cf. 2 Sam. **1.**20). Many of the other references to place-names conceal word-plays or echo knowledge which is now lost to us. 'Dust' (*'aphar*) is found in Beth-le-aphrah (10); Achzib shall become *'achzāb* ('a deceitful thing', 14); Mareshah (15) shall have a 'conqueror' (*yōrēsh*), etc. By this route Sennacherib's army, which has been campaigning against Egypt, will march on Jerusalem, and Judean parents are urged to go into mourning for their children who will be parted from them (16).

Micah 2   Woe to the Oppressor!

In an agricultural community like Israel the possession of land was all-important, and for the small peasant it was a matter of life or starvation. Each citizen had his entitlement to a portion of the city-lands and this had been handed down to him and kept in the family for many generations. This 'portion' (4) or 'inheritance' (2) was regarded as a sacred trust, which he sought to pass on to his children intact. The story of Naboth's vineyard illustrates the Israelite's concern to protect his basic property rights (1 Kings **21.**3), as well as the way in which an unscrupulous tyrant could try to dispossess him. The land-grabbing upper classes of Judah used less brutal means, by foreclosing mortgages, for instance (cf. Amos **2.**6), but the result was that their peasant victims were reduced to poverty and virtual serfdom.

Micah championed the rights of the working-classes and pronounced God's condemnation upon the wealthy ('this family', 3). The men who had without a qualm dispossessed others would be brought under a foreign yoke and would live to bewail the loss of their ill-gotten gains with cries of 'How could God do such a thing?' (4). The city-lands ('fields') would be re-apportioned, and they would get nothing (5).

This was a strong and daring attack on powerful men and it has been suggested that v. 6 was a listener's enraged reply, which Micah takes up and answers (7 f.). In saying 'Is the Spirit of the

Lord impatient?' (lit. 'to be restricted'), he is claiming that nothing is beyond the concern of God: guided by His Spirit the prophet is entitled to investigate and to pronounce on any issue. The upright man will have nothing to fear from his words; only the guilty will react adversely. But then he is the sort who would prefer the prophet to preach under the influence of alcohol rather than of God's Spirit (11)! For their rapacity towards innocent victims (8 f.), these men have defiled the land and will be turned out of it (10). God's land is unclean; it is no longer a place of rest for His people. There is only one solution: the wrongdoer must go, and God has to start again with another 'remnant' (12 f.). The church which is similarly wasted away by dissident elements within it must also take a firm line and part company with them. When the church can no longer be a 'place of rest' for needy men and women, it has ceased to be any use to God.

Micah 3 — The Failure of Judah's Leaders

These words were probably spoken at an important civic occasion in Jerusalem where all the leaders of national life were assembled. Micah begins politely enough (1), but then reverses their standards of good and evil and, before his hearers can decide whether it was a slip of the tongue or not, he accuses them of showing as much consideration for their people as butchers showed to carcasses of meat (2 f.). They were not godless men: they prayed to the Lord (4). But no matter how fervently they prayed, they would get no answer. Sin renders prayer completely useless (cf. Pss. **18.**41; **66.**18).

The prophets receive equally harsh criticism. They are timeservers, and in it for the money (11). They pander to well-to-do clients and have nothing to give to those who are not fee-payers (5). Again, these men are not arrant quacks: they may have been sent by God and known the Spirit's inspiration in days gone by. But now darkness will descend upon them and the genuine prophetic word will be silenced. It is not that God has changed: they have trimmed their sails to the winds of popularity and prosperity. In contrast, Micah claims to have retained the prophetic spirit, which shows itself in divine power, in a sense of justice and in the moral courage to expose the people's sins (8). The true prophet seems always to be aware that he is in the control of the Spirit and is not fully responsible for the words that he speaks (cf. Ezek. **13.**2 f.). Micah's final words (9–12) are a comprehensive indictment of Judah's leadership and this time the priesthood also gets a brief mention (11). In every case the fault is measured in terms of financial gain. Apparently everything (and everybody) has its price: mammon is the measure of all things. Salvation is assured through the presence of the Lord in His holy temple: there appears to be nothing whatever to fear. But Micah makes the shattering statement that inviolable Jerusalem will be razed to the ground: God's house will become a ruin. And it will all be 'because of you', Zion's rulers, whose perversion of truth and justice can be ignored no longer. God's judgement cannot be bought off at any price.

Micah 4.1-8   A Glorious Future for Jerusalem

It is very appropriate that the prophecy of Jerusalem's ruin (3.12) should be followed immediately by this oracle about the place of the new Zion in the last days, when it will serve as the religious metropolis of the whole world. From it the Lord will send forth His law, and many nations will come to learn from His teaching. He will act as Judge of the nations and will inaugurate a period of universal peace when there will be neither arms nor the need for men to leave their homesteads at the call to arms (3 f.). Because vs. 1-3 are almost identical with Isa. 2.2-4, endless discussion has gone on to decide which is original and which is the borrower. In view of the similarity (yet real difference) between Mic. 4.5 and Isa. 2.5, many feel that neither is original, but that both prophets have used a contemporary oracle, modifying the ending to suit their own particular needs. For Micah this appears as a vigorous statement of loyalty to the Lord, when other peoples around are going the way of their own religion. We may be thankful to Micah for his bold commitment, and to Judaism for making this their distinctive witness. If there is any truth at all in the revelation of God, it does not allow for the popular view that one man's religion is as good as his neighbour's. Such tolerance, though highly prized by men of few convictions, is the enemy of the truth. Jesus' claim to be the truth was coupled with His claim to exclusiveness (John 14.6), and this is perfectly logical. The contrast between the ideal future hopes of vs. 1-4 and the present realism of v. 5, where what will be has not yet become a reality, is a perfect example of the delicate balance that all believers must learn to strike between their aspirations and the facts of their experience.

Verses 6-8 continue the theme of the Lord's reign from Mount Zion, but now the main concern is with the mutilated, dispersed flock of Israelites who become the chosen remnant and a mighty force for God. These were later seen to be the exiles in Babylon, but the pattern of God choosing the weak things of the world

and making them great has been repeated continually in human history.
Compare 1 Cor. 1.26–29.

Micah 4.9—5.1   Snapshots of Jerusalem

Here are three pictures of life in Jerusalem at different stages in a siege. Each one begins with the introductory 'now' (9,11; **5.**1). In the first (9 f.) the prophet taunts the inhabitants of Jerusalem for their state of panic. They have a king, the puppet Zedekiah, but he is of little use and the nation is virtually leaderless. They are going through torment and their release from the sufferings of siege warfare will only be to go into exile to Babylon. But there they will find redemption (10). The second picture (11–13) shows the nations gloating over Jerusalem's imminent downfall as they gather round for the pickings. Little do they realize, however, that the Lord has a plan in which they are to be the victims. Jerusalem, instead of being a prey, is a bait to lure them around her. Then, like the sheaves piled around the threshing-floor, the nations will find themselves threshed to pulp under the hoofs of the oxen that tread out the corn, and all the booty taken from them will be devoted to the Lord.

The third is a mere sketch (**5.**1) of a siege-wall built against Jerusalem and the humiliation of Judah's king. The Hebrew is obscure, suggesting a call to mobilize armies (cf. KJV, RV), but the versions are very different (as followed by RSV). The striking of the cheek is an insult which can only be administered to a defeated or humiliated foe (cf. Job **16.**10). While it would not be right to see in Christ's mocking a fulfilment of this prophecy (it is not written as a prediction), the incident of Mark **15.**19 bears a remarkable similarity to this verse and it is clearly more than a coincidence. What Scripture appears to be saying is that Christ bore in His own person all the sufferings of Israel's humiliated king and that the whole of His people's history of rejection was summed up in His Messianic experience.

The chief effect of these three snapshots of Jerusalem is to bring to the situation a new dimension. The people crying out under the sufferings of their siege knew nothing of the redemption that would eventually come; the nations gloating over Jerusalem knew nothing of God's plan to deal with them. God always has His plans; and even though we may not have Micah's insight to know what they will be, it is a great comfort to know that His plan is perfect and it will be worked out.

Micah 5.2-6 The Messiah from Bethlehem

Despite its familiarity from the Christmas lessons, this passage needs explanation because its meaning is not at all clear. In v. 2 God is addressing Bethlehem and saying that, despite its insignificance, it will one day produce another David to rule in Israel. Ephrathah (2) was the name of the district in which Bethlehem was situated (cf. Ruth **1.**2; **4.**11; 1 Sam. **17.**12). The clans (KJV, 'thousands') of Judah were the small administrative districts or 'parishes' which made up rural Judah (like the medieval English 'hundreds'). Among these countless villages Bethlehem had only one claim to fame and that was the antiquity of its link with David, who was its greatest son. Until Bethlehem's history repeated itself in the birth of a Messiah, 'He' (i.e. God) was going to give His people up to their enemies (3a). Only when the travailing woman (= Israel, or the young woman of Isa. **7.**14, or, in the light of Christian fulfilment, the virgin Mary) brought Him forth would the scattered members of the Hebrew community return to the fold and Israel would be unified once more. This aspect of the Incarnation has not yet been fulfilled, but many believe that one day it will and that our Lord's brethren, the Jews, will yet return and the Church, the whole Israel of God, will then be complete (cf. Rom. **11.**23,24,29).

The Messiah's reign will be marked by strength, security, peace and the allegiance of all the earth (4), and in vs. 5 f. Micah gives an example of what this Messianic peace will be like: even the proud Assyrian will be kept at bay and Israel will not lack the leaders to take the war right into the enemy's camp. 'Seven . . . and eight' means an indefinite number of reasonable proportions. To us it seems strange to find the Messianic age of peace expressed in terms of military victory, but for a small nation that was for ever at the mercy of her powerful neighbours this was the only way to security and so to peace. In the coming of Christ, however, we see that this warfare was not against human foes nor was it waged with worldly weapons, but that by the spiritual victory of the cross over His enemies and ours we do indeed find peace.

Micah 5.7-15 Rely only on the Lord

There are two oracles in this section. The first (7–9) consists of two complementary statements about the remnant of Israel and their impact on other nations. They will be like dew, which brings blessing, life and prosperity where it settles (7). They will also be like a lion which destroys and terrifies wherever it goes (8). At first sight contradictory, this pair of similes presents the paradox of Israel's place in the world: a means of blessing and yet a source of judgement; to be welcomed and yet to be feared. The difference between the two aspects is governed by the response of the nations: as they receive the remnant they are blessed, and as they oppose them they are destroyed.

The second oracle (10–15) describes the purifying process which will be applied to Judah in the last days. Everything which could possibly be a substitute for trust in the Lord will be cut off or rooted out: horses and chariots, i.e. military strength; walled cities and fortresses, i.e. military installations; witchcraft and spiritualism, ever-popular alternatives to pure religion (cf. Isa. 8.19 f.). All these were contemporary substitutes for faith in God which were prevalent in Micah's day. Most of all there was idolatry (13 f.), represented by carved images, stone pillars, wooden symbols of the Canaanite fertility goddess Asherah, and sacrificial stones (translated 'cities' in v. 14). All these were the necessary adjuncts of the sex worship of Canaan which was for ever infiltrating the religion of Israel, encouraged no doubt by the fallen nature within every Israelite heart. God saw that the only remedy for this was complete eradication of all evil influences and He promises it to His people 'in that day'. Only then will men be able to trust Him wholly, because 'Satan's sympathizer' will have been finally removed from their hearts.

Snaith points out that all these substitutes for faith reflect what *man* can do; even idols are denounced because they are the work of men's hands (13). This is man's insidious temptation. Trust in his own efforts can frequently hold him back from receiving Christ's salvation by faith, and even the truly converted man can all too easily slip back into forms of self-reliance that cut him off from God's grace. Are we trusting in Him alone—today?

Micah 6.1-8   The Lord's Requirements

Hosea had already used the picture of God bringing a lawsuit against His people (Hos. 4.1; 12.2; cf. Isa. 3.13; 43.26; Jer. 25.31), and here Micah sets the scene with Israel as the defendant and the Lord as both prosecutor and judge. In this cosmic court-room the witnesses are the mountains and the foundations of the earth. Verse 3 begins the prosecution's case, in the form of a survey of Israel's redemption-history from Egypt to the Promised Land. Four aspects only are given a mention: (*i*) the rescue from Egypt, (*ii*) the leadership of Moses, Aaron and Miriam, (*iii*) the reversal of Balaam's intended cursing of Israel and (*iv*) the crossing of Jordan (Shittim being the last main encampment east of Jordan, and Gilgal the first on its western bank). Of particular interest is the Balaam episode, which seems to have had a peculiar fascination for O.T. writers. It occupies three chapters in Num. 22-24 and features in a number of other flashbacks to the wilderness events (e.g. Deut. 23.4 f.; Josh. 13.22; 24.9 f.; Neh. 13.2). Its primary significance seems to be that it showed Israel that God could turn man's evil designs into occasions of blessing, and that neither heathen kings nor hired soothsayers could frustrate God's purposes for His chosen people. For the cult of Balaam in the N.T. (for which a possible Greek translation is 'Nicolaitans'), see a Bible dictionary.

The court-scene now switches to the defendant accepting his guilt and asking what reparation can be made, in terms either of sacrificial offerings or even of the sacrifice of his first-born son (7). But God requires not a gift, but the giver. The good way is expressed in terms of righteous actions, merciful treatment of one's fellow men and living in a humble relationship with one's God. This demands the whole of man: his standards of conduct, his personal relationships and his innermost religious life. Such a fine balance between all three aspects of a man's life could be elaborated, but not improved upon. It is a demand made of every Christian, and to fall short in just one of these items leads to serious spiritual impoverishment. How do we measure up to the Lord's requirements?

Micah 6.9-16   The Merchants of Jerusalem

The Hebrew text of this section is very difficult and the RSV has to make a number of corrections, on the basis of the ancient versions, to make the translation intelligible. The passage is an attack on the traders of Jerusalem who have amassed their 'treasures of wickedness' (10) by dishonest means, viz. with balances that did not weigh fairly and weights that were not up to standard. Micah was not the first to protest against this kind of behaviour (cf. Amos 8.5; see also Deut. 25.13-16; Prov. 20.10), but his words would not have been welcomed. The application of Christian ethical standards to the business-world is rarely appreciated. Many businessmen prefer the Church to keep to the 'spiritual' side of life and to leave them to run their businesses in their own way. Others say that it is impossible to be Christian in the competitive world of modern commerce. The Bible says that God's standards apply everywhere and people who ignore them need not expect to receive His blessing.

The consequences of the dishonesty of Judah and Jerusalem ('O tribe and assembly of the city', 9) are expressed in terms of famine, poverty, death, loss of harvests, devastation of land and being the scorn of other nations (14–16). Moreover, what had already happened to Jerusalem (perhaps in the siege of 701 B.C.) was only the *beginning* of God's punishment (13). Jerusalem's trouble was that she had degenerated so far that she had sunk to the level of Israel in the days of the Omri dynasty (16). Micah may have been thinking specifically of the incident of Naboth's vineyard (1 Kings **21**), but in any case that period had become a byword for apostasy, and now it appeared that Judah was following suit and would therefore merit the prophet's curse on Ahab's house (1 Kings **21**.21 f.). When men turn away from the worship of God it is not long before their private lives are affected as well. Religion and personal morality are more closely related to each other than people care to admit.

A Thought: What observations would Micah have to make about our modern society? or about our private lives?

Micah 7.1-10   From Pessimism to Faith

When a nation lacks good leadership it has no sense of purpose, and without that the people live only for themselves. Politicians use their influence to feather their own nests; lesser officials need monetary persuasion before they will perform their necessary duties on behalf of the public; everyone is somehow on the make. Micah saw a situation like that in the Judah of his day. The nation was like a vineyard after the harvest or as barren as the fig-tree which the Lord cursed (Mark **11**.13 f.). Try as he would he could find nothing of any worth, no godly man to give a lead to the people. Jeremiah, too, was later to look in vain for the same thing (Jer. **5**.1) and the psalmist also despaired over his fellow men (Pss. **14**.1–3; **53**.1–3). Cf. further Isa. **59**.15 f. Micah concluded that the only diligence the leaders of his people showed was to do evil and to take bribes (3). They did not deserve to be reckoned as part of the Lord's vineyard; they were nothing better than highly combustible thorn-bushes that would soon go up in flames (4). So not a soul could be trusted, not even a man's nearest and dearest: the closest family ties were broken in the insane desire for self-advancement.

Had Micah ended at v. 6, we might have suspected him of almost psychopathic pessimism (of the kind that was beginning to infect Elijah in 1 Kings **19**.10), but the following verse restores the balance. The best antidote to a bout of depression is to turn away to the Lord and to be absorbed in Him. Micah looks to Him in *faith*, waits for Him in *patient expectation*, and knows Him as the God who *delivers* him and *hears* his prayer. His final words (8–10) are addressed to his people's enemy, who could be the Assyrians, the Edomites or the Babylonians. He identifies himself with his people and uses 'I' and 'my' to represent the nation. For 'when' in v. 8, translate 'though': however low they may fall, vindication will eventually be theirs through the goodness of the Lord, and the tables will be turned on those who gloated over them (10). R. E. Wolfe in *The Interpreter's Bible* comments that vs. 7–9 are 'like three bouncings of a ball. At the beginning of each it is down, but at the end of each there is a rebound, the rebound of faith'.

Micah 7.11-20   God Forgives

Verses 11–13 are addressed by the prophet to Jerusalem. It is 'a forward look through the clouds of exile to the day when devastated Jerusalem and her walls would be rebuilt' (Wolfe). In faith Micah looks forward to an even more extensive city to which men will come from all parts of the world. Very likely Micah's vision in v. 12 was of the return of Jews who had been dispersed throughout Assyria, Egypt and Babylon ('the River' = the Euphrates), but it is easy to see how Christian readers could interpret these verses of the enlarged new Jerusalem, with its population that no man could number coming from every nation upon earth. Verse 13 indicates that 'the earth' (not 'the land', KJV), i.e. the heathen territories, will be suffering the devastation promised in v. 10.

Verses 14–20 are a concluding prayer to God, as the good Shepherd of His people. It has three parts: (*i*) The prayer that the Lord will come and take possession of His inheritance, and lead them out to pasture 'alone', i.e. without fear of molestation, in the fertile lands of Bashan and Gilead: this will be reminiscent of the miraculous days of the Exodus from Egypt (15). (*ii*) Then the nations of the world will come trembling to the Lord, not in faith, but in fear; their tongues will be silenced, they will be humbled in the dust, and they will submit in abject shame before His mighty power (16 f.). This is not to deny that the nations of the world can believe and come to Zion with singing: the O.T. frequently holds out the hope of the Gentiles' free and spontaneous conversion. Micah, however, was referring to the humiliation of the Gentiles after they had seen (16) the glory of the Lord in His final vindication of His people, when His truth and power would be so forcefully demonstrated that they would have no choice but to acknowledge it. (*iii*) Supremely, God is a God of forgiveness, who loves His children and removes their sins far away, out of *His* sight and out of *theirs* (19). When He punishes, it is only short-lived (18b):but His favour is for a lifetime (cf. Psa. 30.5). This is no new theology, however, but merely the fulfilment of His promises to earlier generations (20). The book that began with the faithlessness of men ends on the note of the faithfulness and goodness of the Lord.

Meditate on vs. 18–20 and make them your own expression of worship.

Questions for further study and discussion on Micah
1. What can we learn from ch. 3 about prayer which is not answered? See especially vs. 4,7; and then turn to 7.7.
2. What does Micah have to contribute to a doctrine of the remnant?
3. With the help of a concordance examine the place of Bethlehem in the O.T. and N.T.
4. What, according to Mic. 3, is the difference between true and false prophets?
5. How did Jesus apply 7.5 f. to the effect of discipleship on His own followers? Study Matt. 10.21,34–38; Mark 13.12; Luke 12.49–53.

Nahum 1   Vengeance and Comfort

Nineveh, the proud capital of the Assyrian empire, fell to the armies of the Babylonians and Medes in the summer of 612 B.C. From that time onwards it became nothing but a heap of ruins, silted up with the sandy deposits of the desert. The modern name for it is Tell Kuyunjik ('mound of many sheep'), which is an unconscious fulfilment of the prophecy of Zeph. 2.13–15.

Nahum probably wrote shortly before this event, predicting it in some of the most graphic poetry the O.T. possesses. He was a Judean, and the suggested location of Elkosh in S. W. Judah is preferable to the traditional association of his tomb with Al-Qûsh near Nineveh. His name means 'comforter' and some have taken this as a kind of *nom de plume* in that, interspersed with his devastating predictions for Nineveh, he incorporates occasional words of comfort for Judah.

Part of ch. 1 consists of an acrostic poem (2–10), but it is not at all easy to disentangle this, and it may be that the author has freely used an older poem without being too concerned to retain its acrostic form. The theme is the avenging wrath of the Lord, though this is interwoven with balancing statements about His patience, justice and goodness to those who trust in Him (3,7).

The presence of both these aspects of God's nature is in itself a reminder to the preacher that his portrait of God must never be overweighted in any one direction. So Nahum looks towards arrogant Nineveh and towards believing Judah at one and the same time.

Comfort for Judah comes out more strongly in vs. 12,13,15. Nineveh, or one of its kings, is addressed in vs. 11,14. (Verse 11 may even be a flashback to the notorious Sennacherib, cf. Isa. **36,37**.) The joyful sequel to Nineveh's fall will be the coming of the messenger of peace, whose arrival in Jerusalem will be the signal for the people to offer the sacrifices that they had promised against the day of their deliverance (15). If the end of an earthly kingdom was to bring such relief and jubilation, how much more welcome should be the good news of the destruction of Satan's empire?

Nahum 2 Storming the Citadel

These verses describe the onslaught of the armies of God upon the ramparts of Nineveh. The troops arrayed for battle present a striking sight with their red shields, scarlet uniforms, gleaming chariots and prancing horses (3, RSV). Before long the outer defences are breached and the battle continues on the city's streets (4). The last stronghold is the temple of Ishtar in the heart of the city, and the attackers are regrouped for the final assault on its walls, using the 'tortoise' siege-engine (known from Assyrian bas-reliefs) as they batter at the defences (5). Then the river-gates are breached and the temple ('palace', AV, RSV) is flooded with torrents of water from the Tigris (6).

Huzzab (7; RSV, 'its mistress') has been taken to be a reference to an Assyrian deity, or the image of one, from its literal meaning of 'that which is set up', but many prefer to emend the text. The associated verbs are feminine and so the idea of a goddess (Ishtar?) being led out in captive procession, followed by her mourning devotees, cannot be discounted. The city (v. 8 is the first mention of Nineveh in the oracle; **1.1** is the title) is emptied of its teeming population (cf. Jon. **4.11**) like a lake drained of its waters, and it becomes a vast treasury of spoil for the conquering army (9).

So ends the glory of Assyria. A final lament over Nineveh makes play upon Assyria's fondness for lion-symbolism in her descriptions of her imperial might. Ishtar herself was often depicted as a lioness or as riding upon a lion's back. But now the lion's den, to which the prey of other nations had often been taken (Israel included; cf. 2 Kings **17.6**), is to be a danger no more. For the Lord is really in control among the nations of the earth. It is His might and His armies which will destroy Assyria. The Babylonian troops who were so soon to invade Nineveh would be His agents, as Habakkuk also observed (Hab. 1.5-11). God is in command and no power on earth can stand against Him. Imagine what a comfort this message was to the little principality of Judah, surrounded as she was by the giant empires of the near eastern world. The struggling community of the Christian Church takes her comfort from the self-same truth.

Nahum 3 — Nineveh's Utter Destruction

This chapter consists of a cycle of prophecies dealing with different aspects of Nineveh's downfall. Verses 1-4 give a fresh description of the battle for the city, in an unusual staccato rhythm that almost catches the sound of the galloping hoofbeats of the attacking chariotry. With this is incorporated a new feature, namely, the reason why she is being treated thus (4). She has seduced other nations by her charms until they are in her power and so, like the harlot that she is, she will receive a harlot's punishment (5-7). She will be exposed and pilloried, and such will be the hatred that she has earned that no one will be found to lament her loss. This is the reward of the prostitute: even her conquests and her customers turn against her in revulsion. Lust knows nothing of loyalty.

Verses 8-13 compare the coming doom of Nineveh with the fate of No-amon, or Thebes, the great city of Upper Egypt, sacked by the Assyrians in 663 B.C. Both cities were founded beside great rivers and both relied partly upon them for defence. Both had vassal territories to turn to for support (9). But Thebes fell and endured the cruel treatment which the Assyrians were notorious for meting out to their enemies; and what could happen to Thebes would happen also to Nineveh (11). The Assyrians would drink deeply of the Lord's cup of wrath; they would reel about drunkenly, seeking a refuge in vain. Their resistance would collapse completely: strongholds would fall and troops would lose their morale (13).

Finally, Nahum ironically exhorts Nineveh to prepare for the siege with supplies of water and bricks (like filling sandbags!). But it will be no use, because fire and sword will do their work no matter what resistance is offered (15). The vast imperial machine of Assyria may appear to be as infinitely powerful as a locust-swarm, but even locusts can disappear overnight (15b-17). There remains nothing more except to pronounce a brief funeral elegy over the Assyrian king, whose generals sleep the sleep of death, whose people are scattered and whose doom is greeted with delight and derision by all (19).

Habakkuk 1 — A Faith that Questions

The abiding value of this little prophecy is that it presents the picture of a man who believes and yet questions. That this is a healthy and not an unspiritual exercise is borne out by the way in which the concluding psalm closes with a towering expression of faith which is scarcely equalled anywhere else in the O.T. (3.17 f.). The key to this outcome is that the prophet questions from a standpoint of initial faith; he takes his questions to God honestly and openly; and he waits upon God for the answers to his problems.

The first question (2–4) deals with God's toleration of oppression. This is similar to the psalmist's 'why do the wicked prosper?' (e.g. Pss. 13; 22; 73). It may refer to the social evils within Judah in Jehoiakim's reign (609–598 B.C.), or it may spring from the time when Assyrian power was at its height under Ashurbanipal (669–626 B.C.). In either case the ability of godless men to tyrannize others unchecked seemed to Habakkuk to be a denial of all the principles of law and justice by which God's world was supposed to be governed. How long could this go on?

The reply comes in the form of an oracle from God (5–11). God's justice is going to be administered by a new power, the Chaldeans, who will trample down oppressors and give them their deserts. This is interpreted variously of Nabopolassar's campaigns of 625 B.C. (freeing Babylon from Assyrian domination) and 612 B.C. (the fall of Nineveh), or of the battle of Carchemish against the Egyptians, in 605 B.C. If Habakkuk's statement was genuinely predictive, this oracle must come from before 625 B.C., and its fulfilment may account for the pro-Babylon sentiments of Jeremiah (Jer. 27.6 f.).

God's reply and the report of its fulfilment raise a second question (12–17): How can a pure God use an instrument as cruel and idolatrous as the Chaldeans? The agents of punishment are even worse than those they are sent to punish (13b). They treat their foes as a fisherman does his catch and they venerate their weapons of destruction (14–16). Is this also to go on for ever? Habakkuk's answer, as we shall see, is that God is entitled to use any means at His disposal to work His sovereign will, but that in the last resort only the man who by faith is righteous will live before Him.

Note: The original in v. 12 has 'Thou shalt not die', corrected by later Hebrew scribes to the more reverent 'we shall not die'. With the following verse this gives us Habakkuk's basic creed: the eternal holiness, goodness and justice of God.

Habakkuk 2   The Fundamental Answer

The prophet sees himself as the spokesman both for the questionings of his fellow Israelites and for the response of God. He does not, however, shoulder the burden of his own complaint. He waits upon God to see what vision will come to him and what answer he is to give (1). Eventually, with a build-up that commits God to the fulfilment of what is to follow (2 f.), the crucial statement comes (4). It deals, not so much with international politics as with the individual's destiny. The wicked man, inflated with his own importance, is not right with God; he is inwardly bent and this will bring about his condemnation and destruction. The righteous man, however, will live (i.e. enjoy abundance of life) through his fidelity.

The word for 'faith' is the Hebrew *'emunah*, meaning 'moral steadfastness' (it is related to 'amen' and to *'emeth*, truth). It is the quality of reliability and loyalty to God's covenant. The person who has *'emunah* is both a man who trusts and a man who is to be trusted. It therefore has both the meanings which can be attached to the Greek equivalent, *pistis*. Paul, in Rom. 1.17; Gal. 3.11, concentrates on the aspect of personal reliance upon God's word which brings justification, but he does not twist the meaning of the Hebrew as some have supposed. In the N.T., as well as in the O.T., life comes through a relationship of faith between man and God.

Verses 6–20 consist of a series of 'woes' addressed to five different classes of evil-doer: the greedy capitalist (6–8), the man who feathers his own nest and imagines himself secure from all retribution (9–11), the ruler who builds cities with the blood and sweat of others less fortunate (12–14), the lascivious man who uses alcohol as a prelude to perversion (15–17), the idolator who worships inanimate objects (18 f.). All these could be veiled attacks on the Assyrians, but it is more natural to see them as denunciations of Judah's sins in the typical prophetic tradition. Verse 20 is probably a liturgical cry which Habakkuk uses to contrast with the sins and idolatry which have gone before, and to prepare the way for the concluding hymn of praise.

For meditation: What place does silent waiting upon God have in your devotional life? Consider the first and last verses of this chapter.

Habakkuk 3   Triumphant Faith

The heart of this psalm consists of a theophany (3–15), as God appears from the southern deserts surrounded by all the awesome features of a violent thunder-storm. Lightning, dark clouds, thunderclaps, torrential rain, all these follow in His wake and bring terror to all mankind. The language is reminiscent of the Sinai appearance to Moses, though Ezekiel was also to use the image of a storm-cloud to introduce his vision of the Lord in Babylon (Ezek.**1.4**). Other poetical passages which bear comparison with Habakkuk's psalm are Deut. 33.2; Judg. **5.4** f.; Pss. **68.**7–16; **77.**16–20. It could be that the prophet is using well-worn symbolism or even an older composition and adapting it to his own needs.

Teman (3) was a district in Edom; Paran was the mountainous area between Edom and Sinai. God was coming from the south, from His Sinai haunts. The fact that the annual rains were usually preceded by the scorching heat of the sirocco, also from the south-eastern deserts, has encouraged some to see the Lord here as the initiator of the annual cycle of fertility—but if so, He is not to be identified with it. The O.T. teaches a God who brings fertility, but not a fertility-god. Traces of ancient mythological figures have been seen in v. 5, named Deber ('pestilence') and Resheph ('plague'; a deity known from Ugaritic texts), but these need not be regarded as anything more significant than literary echoes from the past. (Compare, too, vs. 13 f. with the Babylonian myth of the slaying of Tiamat by Marduk.)

Surrounding this poem are (*i*) the prophet's plea to God to act as Deliverer, as He has done in times past (2), and (*ii*) his terrified reaction to the coming of the Lord in majesty (16). This soon gives way, however, to the affirmation of faith (17–19) that God will be trusted and praised irrespective of the fertility of the crops: He is to be adored for His own sake and not simply for the blessings He brings. If, as some suppose, Habakkuk was a cult prophet, attached to the Temple and taking part in its regular worship, much of his book can be interpreted liturgically. This would explain the question and answer pattern in ch. **1**; the prophetic oracle in **2.**1–4 and the rubric **2.**20; and this psalm as a composition designed for use by the whole community at an agricultural festival. If so, the author's faith would have become the vehicle for strengthening the faith of all the people as they recited it together in the Temple. In this sense we can share with Habakkuk and all Israel in the same expression of trust in God.

Zephaniah 1   The Day of the Lord is Near

The prophet Zephaniah lived in the latter part of the seventh century B.C. and was probably a slightly older contemporary of Jeremiah. His long genealogy (1) suggests noble birth and his great-great-grandfather may well have been the king Hezekiah. To judge from his knowledge of the locality (10 f.), he was a Jerusalemite and he may have been attached to the staff of the Temple. His strictures on idolatry (4–6) suggest that his words were uttered before Josiah's reforms in 621 B.C., which removed most of these abuses from Jerusalem.

The theme running through *Zephaniah* deals with the day of the Lord. This has a long history in Israelite thought, but it was Amos who first confounded his hearers by warning them that it would be a bad day for Israel and not a day of rejoicing. The popular idea that God's people would be blessed abundantly, irrespective of their deserving, was shattered by him once and for all (Amos 5.18–20). Zephaniah speaks in the same tradition: the day of the Lord's judgement is both imminent (7,14) and ruinous (15; cf. too, the frequency of 'I will punish', 8,9,12).

Like Amos, Zephaniah specifies the sins in Judah which merit God's displeasure, e.g. syncretistic worship (4–6), adoption of foreign culture (8), deceit and violence (9), carelessness and complacency (12). As he makes these charges he conducts his hearers on a tour of Jerusalem, beginning with the Temple and the roof-top shrines (4–7), then to the royal palace (8 f.), the commercial centres (10 f.) and finally, roaming the streets, lantern in hand, to those who in their prosperity are indifferent to God (12). The Mortar (11), like 'the hills' (10), is the name of a district of Jerusalem; it was probably a low-lying area, like the 'hollow' of the Tyropoeon valley, where one of the main markets was situated.

The description of men 'thickening upon their lees' (12) implies slothfulness; the phrase relates to wine-making, in which the wine has to be stirred and kept moving by continual pouring from one vat to another or it loses its potency and taste (cf. Jer. 48.11). G. A. Smith comments on this verse: 'God's causes are never destroyed by being blown up, but by being sat upon.' Indifference is the greatest enemy of goodness. Could it have affected you, or your church? If you no longer expect the Lord to do great things, it has.

Zephaniah 2   God's Wrath upon the Nations

Before the prophet turns to pronounce the fate of the heathen he utters a brief, scornful oracle against Judah, the 'shameless nation' (1 f.; this is better than supposing vs. 1–3 to refer to the Philistines). At the same time he exhorts the faithful ('the humble of the land', 3) to seek the Lord's mercy in humble obedience. Clearly there is a chance that the day of the Lord may not be total darkness for everybody. Some in Judah may be saved—'perhaps'. This uncertain prospect becomes more definite later, as a remnant are given specific privileges in vs. 7,9; and a full programme of blessing for them is described in 3.12–20.

The first to experience God's wrath are Israel's age-old enemies, the Philistines (4–7). Only four of the five cities of the Pentapolis are mentioned, Gath having been overpowered in the previous century by Uzziah (2 Chron. **26.6**) and later destroyed by Sargon of Assyria. Cherethites (5) are etymologically the same as Cretans; the Philistines originated from the Aegean islands.

The next oracle is addressed eastwards to the Moabites and Ammonites (8–11), whose arrogance and pride, especially as shown against God's people (and therefore against that people's God), earn them the same fate as the Philistines: devastation and spoliation at the hands of the remnant of Israel. The remaining points of the compass, south and north, are dealt with in vs. 12–15, as Ethiopians and Assyrians are addressed with God's word. In this last oracle Zephaniah augments Nahum's prophecy about the overthrow and utter desolation of the Assyrian capital. From being the pride of a huge empire it will become a place for pasturing flocks, and all kinds of desert creatures (mostly unclean by the standards of Lev. **11**) will haunt its ruins (14). A closing funeral dirge over Nineveh ironically spells out her epitaph in terms, not of her achievements, but of her downfall (15).

These are not simply vindictive predictions of the destruction of Israel's foes. They are to be read as a theological assessment of the world, as seen by God. To the human observer it was chaotic: Israel was weak politically and did little credit either morally or religiously to the faith she stood for. God could not allow this to last for ever. On His day all would be put right: He would be vindicated as sole Ruler of the universe and this meant the overthrow of the mighty, the punishment of unfaithful Israel and the glorification of the righteous remnant. Only so could God be seen to be God. This was what the day of the Lord would achieve.

Zephaniah 3   Corrupt but Purified

There is a marked contrast between the beginning and the end of this chapter. The introductory 'woe' (1) turns to the exhortation to sing aloud for joy (14). In both cases Jerusalem is being addressed. In vs. 1–7, her moral and spiritual breakdown is pronounced in words which show that God must justly punish her guilt. In vs. 11–20, the day of the Lord is seen to produce, not a total overthrow, but only a removal of the guilty members of the community, leaving a righteous remnant to enjoy the salvation and peace of the future Messianic age. Between these two contrasting sections are a pair of shorter oracles, in the first of which (8) the nations of the world are to be destroyed, but this changes in the second (9 f.) to a prediction of their conversion!

It is no solution to this apparent paradox to assume, as many scholars do, that vs. 9–20 are late and not the work of Zephaniah. The combination of the themes of judgement, deliverance of a remnant, and a new life of blessing for the faithful is as old as the story of the Flood. It comes out particularly in the eschatology of the prophets. The day of the Lord has of necessity the two aspects of punishment and purification. If it were only judgement, God's purposes would be utterly frustrated. The remnant *had* to be saved and promised a life of peace and blessing, if God was to remain consistent with Himself. To see any of the O.T. prophets *purely* as a prophet of doom would reflect so badly on his doctrine of God as to be tantamount to denying him his place in the canon. Judgement without mercy is never an attribute of the God of the Hebrews (cf. 5).

For Zephaniah, salvation is for the humble and lowly. This is the quality of quiet dependence on God demanded in Mic. **6.8** and, of course, supremely in *Isaiah* (Isa. **7.9**; **10.20**; **12.2**; **26.3**; **30.15**). It is not far from the faith that Habakkuk looked for (Hab. **2.4**) and the N.T. demanded. Its antithesis is always self-reliance ('your proudly exultant ones', 11), though this may take various forms (e.g. reliance on armies, alliances with other nations, idolatry, etc.). The whole Bible speaks with one voice in saying that salvation is not of works; it is all of God's grace.

Questions for further study and discussion on Nahum, Habakkuk and Zephaniah

1. Summarize the qualities of God which are mentioned in Nah. **1**: how complete is the picture of God given here?
2. What spiritual value is to be derived from the book of Nahum?
3. Examine closely the use made of Hab. **2.4** in Rom. **1.17**; Gal. **3.11**; and Heb. **10.**37 f.
4. What has Habakkuk to teach us, in each of his three chapters, about faith?
5. According to Zephaniah, what will the day of the Lord mean to Judah, to heathen nations, and to 'the humble of the land'?
6. Study the hymn of praise in Zeph. **3.**14–20. Do you see its fulfilment in the experience of the Christian Church, or could it still have meaning for the Jewish people?

Haggai and Zechariah

INTRODUCTION

With these two prophets we move from the seventh to the end of the sixth century B.C. The exile has come and gone. The edict of Cyrus, promulgated after his overthrow of the Babylonian empire in 539 B.C., encouraged the repatriation of foreign prisoners and assisted them with grants towards the re-establishment of their national religious life. The Cyrus Cylinder confirms that the sentiments expressed in Ezra 1.2–4 were the true policy of the new Persian ruler. Haggai and Zechariah were probably among the Jewish exiles who returned with Zerubbabel shortly afterwards. It was many years, however, before the rebuilding of the Jerusalem Temple was seriously taken in hand and it was only the drive and enthusiasm of these two men that saw it through (cf. Ezra 5.1 f.). They prophesied over a brief period of two years, Haggai in 520 B.C. and Zechariah from 520 to 518 B.C. (Zech. 1.1; 7.1).

Haggai 1 The Prophet of Encouragement

Darius I (Hystaspis) succeeded Cambyses on the throne of Persia in 522 B.C., and reigned for 36 years. He appointed, as 'governor' of the newly-constituted province of Judah, Zerubbabel (1), a man who was not only the natural leader of the Jews by virtue of his energy and personality but was also a member of the royal family, being grandson of king Jehoiachin (1 Chron. 3.19). See the *New Bible Dictionary*, s.v. 'Zerubbabel', on the confusion over his father's identity. For this reason Haggai, as well as the people, had great hopes for him as a scion of the Davidic line and he was invested with near-Messianic honours (2.23). Associated with him in leadership was the high priest, Joshua.

Fifteen years before, in 537 B.C., the exiles had celebrated their return by keeping a feast of Tabernacles in the ruins of the burntout Temple and had begun to rebuild it, but opposition and apathy soon halted any progress (Ezra 3.2–4.5). Now Haggai chides the people for devoting their energies to their own houses while the house of God is without a roof and in ruins (4; 'ceiled', KJV, is better than 'panelled'). It is because they have ignored their responsibilities to God that they are suffering bad weather (10 f.), bad harvests (6) and rocketing prices (6b).

The response to the Lord's message through Haggai was quite overwhelming. Seldom has a sermon had such a practical impact. Parties were no doubt organized to get timber from the well-wooded hill country to the south of Jerusalem (8) and this was shaped to provide the spars, rafters and decorative panelling for the Temple, to replace the woodwork destroyed in the fires of 587 B.C. Stonework would have been readily available nearer at hand but this would still need cleaning and re-shaping to any new design (14). Haggai recognized, however, that this was not his doing, but the Lord's; he took no credit for the success of his preaching (12,14). Instead, he encouraged the people with the briefest of oracles (13) to assure them that God was on their side and that they were fellow labourers with Him.

Thought: Christian people need to be reproved and rebuked when they fall short, but they need the ministry of encouragement just as much.

Haggai 2.1-9   The Glory of the New Temple

The number of those in Jerusalem who remembered the glory of Solomon's Temple must have been small. By 520 B.C. many of the older men who were involved in the emotional scenes described in Ezra 3.10–13 would have died. Perhaps it was disillusionment over the delays that prompted the handful that remained to be slightly scornful of the new efforts being made to rebuild God's house (3). Perhaps it was just that greybeards (they must all have been septuagenarians) have a habit of idealizing the past, and these men had forgotten the degradation of Temple worship which Ezekiel had described (Ezek. 8). In any event the criticism of older men can be very dispiriting (and you don't have to be over seventy to live in the past!), and Haggai is prompted to give further incentive to the builders by the promise of God's Spirit among them (4 f.; note the threefold 'take courage'). The promise referred to in v. 5 is not specified and these words are omitted in the Septuagint version, but Exod. 19.5 or 33.14 could be in the prophet's mind; alternatively this is intended to be a general parallel between the Exodus from Egypt and the great new age that is about to dawn.

Verses 6–9 clearly put the immediate future of the new Temple in the context of the end-time. There is the 'shaking of the nations' (6,7; cf. 21 f. and Isa. 13.13; Mic. 1.4), followed by the conversion of the heathen and an era of peace and prosperity (9, where there is probably a play on the meaning of Jeru*salem*, city of peace/*shalom*). The God of the Hebrews is daringly described as the One who owns the riches of the whole world, and these will pour into Jerusalem from all sides so that nothing will be able to rival the new Temple for splendour. That such a claim bore so little resemblance to the actual resources of the struggling Jewish community did not apparently daunt Haggai. He had learnt, as every Christian must, to reckon on God's unseen riches that were available for His people.

The so-called 'Messianic' interpretation of v. 7 ('the Desire of all nations') is based on the Vulgate translation, and is properly abandoned now. The Hebrew demands a plural, 'the desirable things', i.e. the riches of the Gentiles, and in a sense this adds lustre to the overall Messianism of these treasured verses.

Haggai 2.10-23   A Question of Contamination

Within three months of the encouragements offered by Haggai in 1.13—2.9, he appears to be rebuking 'this people' for their uncleanness (14). This seems incongruous to some and they therefore interpret vs. 10–14 as a self-contained oracle relating to the Samaritans, whose offer to assist with the rebuilding of the Temple is rejected by Haggai on the grounds that their uncleanness would be contagious (cf. Ezra 4.1–5). Attractive as this suggestion is, it is unlikely that 'this people' and 'this nation' (14) could refer to any but the Jews, without its being specifically stated, and the addition of vs. 15–19 implies that the writer was thinking of the troubles suffered by the Jewish people before the rebuilding began in earnest. The Samaritan interpretation demands that vs. 15–19 be transposed to just after 1.11 or 1.15 and that the final editor of the book either concealed or failed to realize that the Samaritans were the original subject of the prophecy. In view of this it is probably better to seek another explanation for these words.

The occasion of the oracle is a question put to the priests regarding the relative contagion of holiness ('holy flesh' being the meat of a sacrificed animal) and uncleanness, through contact with a corpse. The answer that the latter is more contagious is turned by Haggai into a parable to show how Israel has been contaminated through her neglect of the ruined Temple. It was like a dead thing in the midst of the city, and it brought upon Israel the troubles described in vs. 16 f. But the point of Haggai's message is that 'from this day on' blessing will come to the people. It is not a rebuke that he is administering so much as an assurance that the days of Israel's chastisement are over. This is followed up by a further message, given the same day (20) and addressed to Zerubbabel, in which he is described as God's servant, His chosen one, and His personal representative ('signet ring'; cf. Jer. 22.24). In view of the military expectations of v. 22 and the expressed hope that in Zerubbabel the Davidic monarchy would be revived, it is not impossible that Zerubbabel's disappearance from the scene shortly after this time was due to Persian suspicions of his loyalty, which brought about his removal from office or an untimely death.

Zechariah 1.1-17   The Four Horsemen

Like John the Baptist, Zechariah began his ministry with a call to repentance. Speaking between the last two prophecies of Haggai (cf. Hag. **2.**1 and **2.**10), he reminded the people of Judah that all their troubles had been due to their fathers' persistent rejection of the message of pre-exilic prophets like Isaiah and Jeremiah (4). So what they needed to do was not simply to rebuild a new Temple: they had to rebuild the foundations of a new society, based on repentance towards God and the sound moral values that the prophets had taught. Zechariah's insistence on these standards of behaviour is one of his chief contributions to the history of his time (cf. Zech. **1.**4; **7.**8-10; **8.**16 f., 19).

In vs. 7-17 we have the first of a series of eight visions. Much of their symbolism is lost on us now, but it is still possible to understand their general import. The background to this first vision could well have been the sight of Persian mounted patrols who acted as the eyes and the ears, as well as the postal service, of the Persian empire. If there was any original meaning in the colour of the four horses, it is lost to sight. We are not justified in reading the interpretation given in Rev. **6** back into this vision. Zechariah has the assistance of a divine messenger, 'the angel who talked with me', who acts as the mouthpiece of God Himself in interpreting to the prophet what he sees. The horsemen are God's patrols reporting that all is peaceful upon earth (11).

This news dismays 'the angel of the Lord', presumably yet another angelic figure, who appears to be disappointed that nothing more spectacular is happening to Jerusalem after the seventy years prophesied by Jeremiah (Jer. **25.**12) have nearly come to an end (i.e. 587 B.C. to the present, 520 B.C.). It looks as if the upheavals in the Persian empire which followed the death of Cambyses and the accession of Darius I (522 B.C.) had been interpreted as signs of the inauguration of the Messianic era (cf. the shaking of the nations, Hag. **2.**6, 21 f.). Darius' success in subjugating his empire was a real disappointment. However, this is compensated by a series of favourable statements ('gracious and comforting words', 13) about God's concern for Jerusalem (14), His displeasure with

Jerusalem's enemies (15), the promise of the city's rebuilding (16) and her eventual prosperity (17).
Let all our disappointments lead us to the promises of God.

Zechariah 1.18—2.5   Jerusalem's Protection

There are two separate visions here, but both of them relate to the Lord's protection of Jerusalem. In the first (1.18-21) the four horns represent heathen powers hostile to Judah. Their number signifies completeness, as if coming from the four corners of the earth (cf. the four horsemen of 1.10 and the four chariots of 6.5 f.). For the horn as a symbol of power, compare 1 Kings 22.11; Jer. 48.25. To meet these the Lord produces four smiths, who are meant to represent His agents of destruction upon the oppressor nations. Commentators refer to Ezek. 21.31 where the phrase 'skilful to destroy' translates what is literally 'smiths of destruction'. These will 'terrify' the nations, thus repaying them in their own coin, and render them powerless.

Note that this is entirely the Lord's provision for His people. He intervenes on their behalf and provides His own agents and weapons against their foes. The number of the smiths is also intended to be a reminder that God's resources exactly match the needs they are meant to satisfy. He does not have to be extravagant in His provision for our needs, but He never underestimates them. His power is 'sufficient for every need'.

The second vision is reminiscent of the angel in Ezekiel's vision of the new temple (Ezek. 40.3); but it is doubtful whether Zechariah meant the man with a measuring-line to be understood as an angelic figure. This would mean that there were three angels in this one brief scene (cf. 2.3). Possibly this is a self-conscious autograph (in the same way as the young man of Mark 14.51 f. probably was), and the prophet is addressing the message to himself. Alternatively, it could be Zerubbabel.

The message is that the city of Jerusalem needs no walls to protect it; partly because it will be so populous that it will overflow them anyway, and partly because the Lord is going to dwell in the midst and be her Protector (cf. Rev. 21.23,25). This is a great spiritual truth which the builders of Jerusalem took to heart, but the pressing need for protection against outside interference eventually led Nehemiah to fortify Jerusalem in *c.* 444 B.C. Perhaps it is no accident that the period of Ezra–Nehemiah moulded Judaism into a religion of exclusiveness from which it has never been released.

Walls can imprison those within, as well as keeping others out.
Meditation: Are we in danger of building walls around God?

Zechariah 2.6-13   A Call to Return Home

It is clear from v. 7, as well as from the narrative in *Ezra–Nehemiah*, that many Jews stayed in Babylon after the decree of Cyrus and failed to take advantage of the offer of repatriation which was held out to them. Many of them had, of course, been born in exile and had so come to terms with their environment that they would not face the upheaval of the journey and the uncertainties of settling into a completely new way of life in Judah. An enthusiastic call from one who had made the effort, like Zechariah's plea in these verses, might have swayed the minds of some. The situation has its parallel in the unwillingness shown by the Israelites to venture out of Egypt into the Promised Land and, in Christian terms, of the slowness of many an unbeliever to be persuaded to step out into faith and eternal life.

Zechariah first appeals to the exiles still in Babylon to return to Jerusalem and to escape the judgement which is about to fall on that country (6–9). The 'land of the north' (6) is a vague reference to their land of exile and may carry echoes of the mythological Saphon, the home of the Canaanite gods, which is a cognate of the Hebrew for 'north'. Evil nearly always struck from that direction; it was the direction from which the sun never shone. The original reading of v. 8 had 'My eye', but this was altered to 'His eye' because it was thought to represent too anthropomorphic a picture of God. The thought that anyone who harmed God's people was touching God in His most sensitive part is a very striking one.

In vs. 10–12 the people living in Jerusalem are addressed. For them there will be nothing but blessing. The Lord will dwell in their midst and heathen peoples will come and share their allegiance to Him. Their land will be 'the holy land' (12), the only time, incidentally, in the O.T. when this name is given to Palestine. Verse 13 looks like a liturgical formula (cf. Hab. 2.20), borrowed for the occasion to show that God is about to take action very soon to reveal His glory. When that happens and these predictions are fulfilled, Zechariah's prophetic calling will be authenticated (9,11). How many people know that the Lord has sent us?

Zechariah 3   The Vision of Joshua's Cleansing

The fourth and fifth visions are concerned with Judah's leadership, in the persons of Joshua and Zerubbabel. In this chapter it looks as if charges had been made against Joshua concerning his unfitness for high priestly office. This may have come from those who had remained in Judah and who felt that Joshua had been polluted by his residence in Babylon. Equally, Joshua may have stayed in Judah during the exile and been accused of compromise by those who returned. Certainly there was a deep rift which Zechariah's vision was intended to heal.

The vision is of the Lord's tribunal (cf. Job 2.1), with Satan (lit. 'the accuser') fulfilling his customary role as the prosecutor of God's people. By command of the angel of the Lord (who appears to be the personification of the Lord Himself) Joshua's filthy robes are removed and he is clothed in clean garments and invested with clean priestly headgear. This symbolical authentication of Joshua's status is confirmed by the words that follow (6–10). In these Joshua and his fellow priests are given 'right of access' to God's heavenly court on condition that they observe God's moral laws ('walk in My ways') and follow the priestly duties ordained by Him ('keep My charge' being a cultic term, cf. Ezek. 44.15 f.). If they do this they are given jurisdiction in the renewed Temple, and God will establish His Messianic servant, the Branch, a title which must obviously refer to Zerubbabel (based on Isa. 11.1; Jer. 23.5 f.; 33.14–16).

The stone with seven 'eyes' or facets has been variously interpreted (9). The least improbable suggestions are that this was (*a*) a jewel in the Messiah's diadem on which would be inscribed Zerubbabel's name; (*b*) a symbol of the completed Temple in the form of an inscribed coping-stone; (*c*) a precious stone to be worn on the high priest's person, similar to the breast-plate jewels or the turban inscription of Exod. 28.9–12,36–38. That these events will genuinely herald the Messianic age is borne out by the closing references to the removal of sin (9b) and the idyllic life of peace and security, borrowed from Mic. 4.4.

It need not deter us that Zechariah's expectation that the new age was about to dawn was not fulfilled. An imminent Messianism has always been the mark of a healthy church, in both O.T. and N.T. times, as well as in the present day. God frequently allows us to have our hopes, but then shows that the best is yet to be.

Zechariah 4   The Lamp and the Olive Trees

In order to understand the meaning of this vision one must first separate off the paragraph from 'This is the word of the Lord' (6) to 'in the hand of Zerubbabel' (10a). The rest of the chapter then flows in an intelligible sequence. If we look at the two sections separately we can then see how they relate to each other.

The vision proper (1–6a, 10b–14) is of a gold, seven-branched lampstand, the seven lamps being supplied with oil from a central bowl or reservoir (2). The seven lips are the nozzles which hold the wicks. Flanking this are two olive trees which appear to be supplying the oil to the reservoir by means of two golden pipes (12). Alternatively, the pipes are simply the channels by which the central bowl feeds the lamps, and the olive trees are worked in gold on either side of the bowl just beside its two outlets.

The interpretation is not without its difficulties. Some see the lampstand (which has many similarities with the one described in Exod. **25**.31–37) as a symbol of the Lord, and this is attested by the comparison of the lamps with the seven eyes of the Lord in v. 10b. If this is correct, it would be impossible to interpret the olive trees as if they were *supplying* the oil for the lampstand. God does not need His anointed ones as much as that! They would have to be thought of as His servants, standing by His side and dependent upon Him. Another interpretation makes the lampstand a symbol of the Jewish community, through whom God surveys the whole earth (10b) and who are supported and sustained by God's two appointed and anointed leaders, Joshua and Zerubbabel, who act as the channels of divine grace to His people. A third alternative, based on the cultic significance of the lampstand, is to see it as a symbol of the Temple, which is sustained by the Spirit of God through His two servants and which serves as the eyes of God in the earth. The passage in Rev. **11**.4, based upon these verses, develops a symbolism of its own and does not help with the interpretation of Zechariah's vision.

The parenthetic passage (6b–10a) relates to Zerubbabel and the Temple, assuring him that his problems will be overcome and that the building will be completed amid general acclamation (7,9). The plummet (10) will be in his hand as he lays the last stone straight and true. These verses have only a general connection with the vision, though their concern with the Temple suggests the third alternative interpretation as the likeliest. They also link the supply of oil to the lampstand with the resource of God's Spirit (6b) and this is a significant identification. To displace this section to after **3**.10 or **6**.15, as many would wish to do, does not make things any easier, and it seems best to keep it in its context, either as a large parenthesis or as following on from **4**.14.

Meditate on v. 6 in relation to your Christian service.

Zechariah 5 — The Removal of Sin

These two visions are an elaboration of the promise made in 3.9b, that God will remove the iniquity of the land. They follow naturally upon the visions which deal with the purifying and authorization of the nation's leadership. Two methods of purging are reflected in the visions. In the first (1–4), evil men are exterminated by means of a curse written upon a huge flying scroll, measuring 30 ft. by 15ft., which hovers over the land of Judah and settles upon individual habitations. This is a strange figure to our minds, but it reflects the Hebrew concept of the effective power of the curse in dealing with the individual wrongdoer. Other judgements affected groups of people, but the terms of a curse could be specific and it would therefore touch only those specified. Compare the cursings (or 'sanctions') which were an integral part of ancient covenants, e.g. Deut. **27**.15–26; **28**.15–19.

The measurements of the scroll do not have any recognizable significance, except to show that it was unrolled and of tremendous size. No reader of *Zechariah*, for instance, would remember that it had the same dimensions as the porch of Solomon's Temple. Comparisons of this sort can only lead to fanciful exegesis. The two kinds of wrongdoer mentioned in vs. 3 f. are representative of those who commit sins against their fellow men rather than against God.

The second vision (5–11) envisages the physical deportation of wickedness, personified as a woman, in a large measuring-bowl or barrel ('ephah') with a leaden lid. She is carried off by two other women with stork-like wings and deposited in Babylon (Shinar), where a temple is built for her. The context suggests that the woman represents the sin of idolatry, which is to be cleared out of Judah and banished (appropriately) to Babylon, where a suitable welcome will await her. The word 'base' (11) is normally used for the pedestal of an idol or altar. Taken this way this vision complements the previous one and promises the removal of religious as well as social sins.

Meditate on Psa. 51.1–4.

Zechariah 6 — The Four Chariots

The series of eight visions concludes with one reminiscent of the first (cf. **1**.8–17). The horsemen are replaced by chariots, because whereas the former were patrols reporting back with information about the state of affairs on earth, the chariots are hostile agents with the task of executing God's wrath upon the people of the north country, i.e. upon Babylon (8). Once again there are problems over the colours of the horses, and occasional inconsistencies if they are compared too closely with **1.8**, but it is better that we admit our inability to understand it all than that we follow the Greek version in harmonizing everything into a pleasing kaleidoscope. The only clear meaning is that given in v. 8, namely that God's anger against Babylon has been satisfied in the punishment of its inhabitants, and so the wrongs done to His people in the exile have now been fully avenged. 'Spirit' (8) has the meaning of 'anger', as in Judg. **8.3**; Prov. **16.32**.

Verses 9–15 represent the symbolic crowning of Joshua the high priest, as a kind of historical appendix to the visions. But there are problems: (*a*) why should Joshua and not Zerubbabel be crowned? (*b*) why is Joshua now called the Branch (12)? (*c*) what is the meaning of 'between them both' (13)? The fact that the Hebrew has 'crowns' instead of the singular in vs. 11,14 suggests to most commentators that this was originally written with the names of both Joshua and Zerubbabel in v. 11. Then vs. 12,13a would describe the coronation of Zerubbabel, the Messianic ruler and builder of the Temple, and v. 13b would refer to Joshua, who would be Zerubbabel's religious counterpart and would govern harmoniously with him. The very writing down of this prophecy would have been like an act of treason against the Persian authorities and it may even have contributed to Zerubbabel's downfall. If this was indeed so it is not surprising that his name had been removed from the book for political reasons, but traces of the original prophecy were left behind so that the perceptive could read between the lines. Verse 10 suggests that recent reinforcements had arrived from Babylon (cf. **2.6 f.**), bringing with them these offerings for the new Temple.

For consideration: How can you 'help to build the temple of the Lord' (15)? See Eph. 2.22; 1 Pet. 2.4–6.

Zechariah 7   A Question about Fasting

By 518 B.C. the work on the Temple must have been making real headway. At this point a deputation arrived from Bethel to ask about the necessity for continuing the fasts which commemorated the sack of Jerusalem. The fifth month (3) was the month in which the city had been burnt by the Babylonians (Jer. **52.12 f.**). In the seventh month (5) Gedaliah, the Babylonian nominee, had been murdered by Ishmael (2 Kings **25.25**). Bethel was in the northern province, though only twelve miles north of Jerusalem, and its inhabitants would have been the mixed population, settled there by the Assyrians, who were later called Samaritans. Zerubbabel showed them no great friendliness (see Ezra 4.1-3) and this may be why Zechariah rebuffed the deputation. It is not easy to see why Bethel, which had long set itself up as a rival to Jerusalem, should have sought the authoritative ruling of the priests and prophets of that city. Perhaps their intentions were not wholly sincere.

In his reply (4-7) the prophet questions the value of the fasts, implying that they had been directed manwards and not Godwards. Fuller consideration of the teaching of the pre-exilic prophets might have saved the people of Bethel from their concentration on matters of ceremonial at the expense of moral righteousness (7.9-12). The fast which God was pleased with is that described in Isa. 58.6-10. Moreover, these fasts (and two more are mentioned in 8.19) were initiated to enable the people to lament their losses, i.e. they were for their own satisfaction and they had been occasioned by their own disobedience (11 f.). T.C. Speers (Interpreter's Bible) comments: 'A fast is a means to an end. . . . Religion and all religious practices exist for the sole purpose of establishing a closer, more meaningful relationship between people and God.' This should be the criterion by which everything we do in God's name is to be measured.

Verses 9 f. summarize the O.T. standard of justice. This is very different from Roman *iustitia*, represented by the blindfold goddess with a balance and a sword. It meant fair dealings for all men, but with a particular element of consideration for the deprived member of the community. To the Hebrew mind, justice and mercy were bound up with each other, a fact demonstrated supremely in the cross, where God could be 'just and the justifier' (Rom. 3.26).

Question: What part should fasting play in the Christian's life, and what safeguards should be applied?

Zechariah 8.1-13   Bright Hopes for Jerusalem

This chapter consists of ten prophecies concerning the era of salvation which is about to dawn upon Jerusalem. All are introduced with 'Thus says the Lord (of hosts)', as in vs. 2, 3, 4, 6, 7, 9, 14, 19, 20, 23. Most of them make reference to the glorious future of the holy city, and several echo earlier statements made by Zechariah.

(*i*) Verse 2 is virtually a repeat of 1.14: God's jealousy includes His ardent zeal *for* Jerusalem and His anger *against* her enemies.

(*ii*) Verse 3 is similar to 1.16; 2.10, and echoes Isa. 2.2: God would return to Jerusalem and inhabit it once again, as envisaged in Ezek. 43.1-5.

(*iii*) Verses 4 f. present the combined blessings of ripe old age for the inhabitants of Jerusalem and of many children playing freely in the streets (cf. Isa. **65.**20, 23). This symbolizes freedom from war, sickness and famine, which were the great decimators of human life. In O.T. times, when there was no bright prospect of an after life, longevity was a blessing greatly to be prized (cf. 2 Chron. **1.**11).

(*iv*) Verse 6 reflects the doubts that some felt about Zerubbabel's ability to carry through his ambitious plans (cf. Hag. **2.**3; Zech. **4.**10). What they thought to be too wonderful to be true, however, God could regard as wonderful *and* true.

(*v*) Verses 7 f. are a well-used statement of God's intention to restore the scattered community of Judah from their various places of exile. 'East' and 'west' mean more than just Babylon and Egypt. All will return to become once again God's covenant people in a relationship of mutual trust ('faithfulness' = reliability) and harmony ('righteousness' is the word used when both parties to a covenant are keeping it properly).

(*vi*) Verses 9–13 are a more elaborate exhortation, designed to encourage the work of building by showing the change in the fortunes of Judah since the work began. The economic distress of the early days is giving way to fruitfulness and fertility (12), and even the nations will bless themselves by Israel (cf. Gen. **12.**2 f.; **22.**18). It is a striking thought that, when God really blesses those who put their trust in Him, even unbelievers will notice and appreciate it.

Zechariah 8.14-23　　　　The Question Answered

(*vii*) Verses 14–17: Zechariah is emphatic that in the good days that are coming the ethical demands of God are not to be forgotten. There is no sense in which he is thinking of an age where sin is a human impossibility. Even though God gives His people peace, they are still to make judgements that 'make for peace' (16). This reduces the level of Zechariah's expectation from the full Messianic 'golden age', described in Isa. **11.**1–9, for instance, to that of an age of salvation. We would compare it with the post-Pentecostal era, when salvation is a reality and God is with His people by His Spirit, as against the sin-free perfection of heaven, which is yet to come.

(*viii*) With vs. 18 f. we come at last to the answer to the deputation's enquiry (7.3). The two fasts that are added probably commemorated the date when the siege of Jerusalem had begun, in the tenth month (i.e. January 588 B.C.; cf. 2 Kings **25.**1); and the date when the Babylonian army breached the walls some eighteen months later, in the fourth month (2 Kings 25.4). In the spirit of the new age, Zechariah advocates turning these into feast days, because rejoicing is in future to be the hallmark of the Hebrew community. One wonders whether his words were consciously in our Lord's mind when He made some of His observations on fasting, e.g. Matt. 9.14 f. Jesus was very aware that He was ushering in the age of salvation that had long been expected.

(*ix*) Verses 20–22 fill out the statement in 2.11a about the influx of Gentiles into the saved community. All men will enthusiastically want to share in the Lord's blessings upon Jerusalem and will encourage each other to take part. Gentiles will be the evangelists to lead other Gentiles to God. They will not come patronizingly, for they will see that they have no claim upon the God of the Hebrews; they will come, as they rightly should, to seek His favour.

(*x*) The last of this decalogue of prophecies foretells the tenfold expansion of the Jewish faith as every Jew brings with him ten Gentiles who are anxious to accept his way of life. The phrase 'God is with you' recalls the Immanuel prophecy (Isa. 7.14; cf. 45.14), and looks forward to the day when a Jew will draw all men to Himself (John 12.32).

Questions for further study and discussion on Haggai and Zechariah 1–8

1. What does Haggai 1.4 have to say to us on the relative priorities of our home and our church?
2. What incentives did Haggai give to the people to encourage them to work for God?
3. What place does the Holy Spirit have in the writings of these two prophets?
4. From what sins did Zechariah feel his people needed to be cleansed? See 1.1–6; 3.1–9; 5.1–11; 7.1–7.
5. Consider the passages which attach Messianic status to Zerubbabel, e.g. Hag. 2.23; Zech. 3.8–10; 4.7–10; 6.11–13. Do these justify us in regarding him as a type of Christ?
6. With the help of a concordance, collect all the O.T. references to Satan. What does his chief role appear to be?
7. How did Zechariah draw upon the teachings of his predecessors, the prophets before the exile?

Zechariah 9-14

INTRODUCTION

The last ten chapters of the O.T. consist of three groups of material, each beginning with the word 'Oracle' (Zech. **9.**1; **12.**1; Mal. **1.**1). The third is named after Malachi (lit. 'my messenger') which may simply be the subject of the oracle (see Mal. **3.**1) and not a personal name. The others are added on to the end of *Zechariah* without any explicit mark of identification. To assume that they are *not* by Zechariah, as many critics do, and to attribute them to a supposed 'Deutero-Zechariah' does not help at all. It glosses over the real similarities that exist between chs. **1–8** and **9–14** (for a list of these see the *New Bible Dictionary*, s.v. 'Zechariah, Book of', p. 1356), and it is never satisfactory to argue from a change of style to different authorship. Certainly, Zech. **9–14** are in a markedly different literary category from **1–8**: they are apocalyptic, and they do not deal with the rebuilding of Jerusalem or the progress of the Persian empire. But they are virtually impossible to date from internal evidence alone, and that is all there is to go on. They do, however, contain an effective message, which will be our main interest in the comments that follow. On the question of authorship we can only say that they could be by Zechariah, they have traditionally been attributed to him, but they do not claim to be and it does not matter greatly if they are not his work.

Zechariah 9 The Triumph of the Messiah

One of the strongest marks of similarity between the two halves of *Zechariah* is in their concept of the Messianic age: both of them concentrate their attention on its imminence, and chs. **9–14** lead on from many of the expectations of chs. **1–8**. The main difference is that Zerubbabel is well out of the picture in chs. **9–14**, and these chapters must have been written after he had been discredited (presuming that was his fate). The Messianic hope still burns brightly, however, and in ch. **9** we see the awaited King's triumphal march on Jerusalem (9).

This is preceded in vs. **1–7** by a description of an army invading from the north, defeating first Syria (Hadrach, Damascus and Hamath), then Phoenicia (Tyre and Sidon), and finally Philistia (Ashkelon, Gaza, Ekron and Ashdod). Some would see this as a prophecy relating to Alexander's march southwards after defeating the Persians at the battle of Issus (333 B.C.). But in view of the expectation that Philistia would become a satellite of Judah, embracing the Jewish faith and sharing the remnant's privileges (7), this interpretation is most unlikely. While other nations would be overrun, God would see to it that His house was protected by His own presence (8). The Jebusites (7) were the ancient inhabitants of Jebus (= Jerusalem) who were assimilated after David's victory (2 Sam. 5.6 ff.).

The triumph of God's anointed King reaches its climax as He enters Jerusalem, not on a prancing charger surrounded by His men of war, but in lowly dignity riding upon an ass (9). His reign is going to be marked by compulsory disarmament, by a rule of peace (10) and by release for all Hebrew captives (11 f.). The justification for this is to be found in the covenant of Sinai, which was sealed by the sprinkled blood (Exod. 24.6–8), and is therefore binding upon God as well as upon His people (11). So the Lord will give His people superiority over their foes, protection from all troubles and prosperity and honour in their new life (13–17). The reference to Javan (Greece, v. 13) has been thought to be a gloss, added after the Greeks came to power under Alexander, but Greece appears in earlier passages (e.g. Isa. 66.19; Ezek. 27.13; Joel 3.6) as a distant power to be reckoned with.

Summarize the blessings which come to the Christian through the triumph of Christ, and claim them for yourself.

Zechariah 10   The Need for Proper Leadership

Our Lord's pity for the multitude because they were 'like sheep without a shepherd' (Matt. 9.36; Mark 6.34) recalls sentiments expressed in several O.T. passages (e.g. Num. 27.17; Ezek. 34.5) where God saw the need of His people for strong spiritual leadership. Because they were leaderless, the Jewish people in the time of which Zechariah was speaking were being led astray to seek the blessing of rain and fertility for the crops through all kinds of superstition (2). Clearly Zerubbabel, and probably Joshua, too, were by now no longer at the helm. Teraphim were the household gods, highly prized from ancient times (Gen. 31.19; Judg. 17.5, etc.) but frequently associated with divination (2 Kings 23.24; Ezek. 21.21). Despite the O.T. prohibitions of these and other forms of spiritualism, the fact that Hebrew had an extensive vocabulary of words relating to its practice and its practitioners suggests that it was much more widespread than would otherwise appear. Its fault was that it interposed magical or demonic powers between the inquirer and God, who alone should be approached and consulted direct (1; cf. Isa. 8.19).

The shepherds and leaders of v. 3 may well be foreign overlords, but God promises to overthrow them (11) and to make Judah strong under native leadership ('out of them', 4). At that time all the pre-exilic threats would be reversed; instead of Israel's rejection there would be acceptance (6); instead of defeat, victory (5,7); instead of dispersion, return and redemption (8-10). As with a number of other similar passages (e.g. Isa. 43.16-19; 48.20 f.), Israel's return, whether from the Babylonian exile or from the dispersion which followed Alexander's conquests, is seen in terms of a second Exodus from Egypt through the waters of the Red Sea (11). This great act of redemption was as definitive for Israel as the cross is for the Christian Church. It is no accident that in the N.T. Christ's ministry and death are frequently understood in 'Exodus' terms (Luke 9.31, etc.).

Zechariah 11   The Shepherd of the Flock

The opening verses (1-3) continue the theme of the previous chapter and are a mock lamentation over the fall of the tyrants who had been dominating Israel. Cedars of Lebanon and oaks of Bashan were symbols of great powers, as in Isa. 2.13; 10.33 f.; Ezek. 31.1-18. Similarly their rulers were described as shepherds and lions (3).

Verse 4, however, introduces a new theme. The prophet is bidden to act the part of shepherd of God's flock, but he in turn is in the employ of unscrupulous master-shepherds who care nothing for the flock and exploit it for their own profit (5). He takes on the job and his intentions are symbolized by the two staffs named 'Grace' (i.e. God's covenant with the flock) and 'Union' (i.e. harmony between Israel and Judah). His destruction of three shepherds in one month (8, a historical allusion which has been variously interpreted) does not win him the loyalty of the flock, who apparently prefer being exploited to being cared for. So the covenant is annulled (10) and the prophet asks to be paid off (12). The 'lordly price' of thirty silver shekels changes hands (surely said scornfully—it was a slave's value, Exod. 21.32) and he deposits it in the Temple treasury where, as he was acting in God's name, it rightly belonged.

There is a variant reading in v. 13, recognized by RSV margin, and it is interesting that in the Gospel narrative where this is applied to the betrayal price of Jesus, both traditions are remembered (Matt. 27.5-7). So the money is both offered to 'the treasury' (Heb. *hāʾōtsar*) and used to buy the field of 'the potter' (Heb. *hayyōtser*).

The prophet is here representing God, who comes to His people with the twin blessings of covenant and unity. The people, however, reject His offer and so the cancellation of these gifts must be their responsibility. Finally, the prophet is told to play the role of a worthless shepherd, for that is the kind of leadership the people are going to have to endure (15 f.).

A dogmatic interpretation of these words is impossible. They cannot refer to the Messianic age and they appear to have no real link with what has gone before. They do, however, have remarkable similarities with the coming of Jesus Christ, His rejection by the people He came to shepherd, His betrayal by Judas. But details must not be pressed or Jesus will be found to be His own betrayer. Probably the original meaning had to do with an immediate historical situation which our scanty knowledge of the period prevents us from understanding in any detail.

Thought: 'Grace and Union—two of Christ's most precious gifts to His people.' How would you interpret them?

Zechariah 12 — The Martyred Messiah

With these closing chapters we meet with the apocalyptic style of writing for the first time in *Zechariah*. Notice the frequency of the phrase 'On that day' (3, 4, 6, 8, 9, 11; **13.1**, etc.), found previously only in **9.16**. This sort of writing is futuristic, symbolical and often cryptic. It deals with the last days but is often addressed to the present. One commentator describes it as 'a pep-talk to the faithful and a nightmare to the sober expositor'.

The main theme is the inviolability of Jerusalem. The Lord is on her side and will strengthen her inhabitants so that they will be able to devastate the hostile peoples round about (2–6). In the final battle with the nations of the world, which is a recurrent theme in apocalyptic writings (cf. Ezek. **38,39**; Rev. **12**, etc.), the tribes of Judah will realize that supernatural forces are at work on behalf of the people of Jerusalem (5) and will fight more ferociously and successfully than they (7). In this way Jerusalem and her Davidic house will be rebuked for their arrogance, but this is to be only temporary: a Davidic ruler of semi-divine status will arise to lead the people to final victory and the nation will become strong and glorious (8 f.).

At the height of the triumph, however, there is introduced a note of sombreness. Mourning and lamentation will fill the land like the mourning at the first Passover (if that is the meaning of 'over a first-born' in v. 10) or like the ritual weeping of the heathen over their dying vegetation-gods (11; cf. Ezek. **8.14**). The reference to the plain of Megiddo has been associated with Josiah's untimely death there (2 Kings 23.29), but it may simply have been the site of this Canaanite ritual. Nathan and Shimei were sub-clans of David and Levi.

The cause of this mourning is the violent death of an unnamed hero, who could be the prophet himself but is more likely the Davidic king, over whom the people feel remorse as well as sorrow, inasmuch as they had been responsible for his death (10). Numerous attempts have been made to find a historical context for this prophecy, but none is so apt as that which sees in it a prediction of the cross. Could it be that one day the Jewish people will feel remorse and come to repentance and faith in their crucified Messiah?

Let your prayers today include a prayer for the conversion of the Jews.

Zechariah 13   Cleansing for God's People

If, as seems likely, these verses follow on from the end of ch. 12, it appears that Zechariah intended us to see a relationship between the Messiah's martyrdom and the cleansing of the house of David from its sin (1). There is also more than an echo of the language of Isa. 53, quite sufficient indeed to make these parts of *Zechariah* a regular treasure-chest for the prophetic interpreters of the apostolic Church. To judge from Matt. 26.31 (= Mark 14.27), this was a lesson they learned direct from our Lord, who must have used these Scriptures, alongside Isa. 53, to develop His own sense of being the Shepherd of His flock, the King of peace, the pierced Messiah and the means of His people's cleansing. All of these crucial concepts lie concealed in chs. 9–14 of *Zechariah*.

Verses 2–6 show that in the last days even prophecy will have become discredited. It will be classed with idolatry (2); prophets will disavow their calling (5) and be disowned by their families (3); and they will avoid wearing their distinctive uniform (4; cf. 2 Kings 1.8; Matt. 3.4). Verse 6 probably means that prophets who have suffered lacerations in an ecstatic frenzy (cf. 1 Kings 18.28) will pretend that they were simply scratches received in a friendly brawl. This is, of course, not true prophetism, but a totally false phenomenon which is a parody of the real thing. An alternative interpretation is to regard the prophet in v. 6 as a true prophet who has been persecuted by his friends for following his vocation, and whose injuries thus received belie his claim to be a simple tiller of the soil. This explanation fits in better with attempts to read back Christ's scourging into this verse, but it agrees less readily with the context of discredited prophets.

Verses 7-9 deal with the Messianic testing, i.e. the purificatory sufferings which precede the dawn of the age of Messianic bliss. The shepherd is here a good leader (unlike 11.15-17), who is smitten in order that the flock may be scattered and subjected to the fires of persecution. Only a third will survive, but they will be the remnant who will inherit the covenant blessing of being God's special possession (9). So when Christ came He was at pains to show that the reign of universal peace was *not* imminent. There would be wars, persecutions and suffering (e.g. Matt. 10.34).

For study: what does the Bible say about the value of persecution? See Job 23.10; Isa. 48.10; Mal. 3.3; 1 Pet. 1.7.

Zechariah 14   A Glimpse of the Age to Come

Again, in typical apocalyptic style, the curtain that hides the future from sight is drawn back for a few brief glimpses into the happenings of the last days. The chapter has little cohesion apart from this, and it ranges over an onslaught on Jerusalem (2), with the inhabitants escaping through a rift in the Mount of Olives (4 f.); a transformation of nature (6-8); the establishment of God's kingdom (9); the levelling of the hill-country around Jerusalem (10 f.); a plague on Jerusalem's enemies (12-15), and the enforced conversion of those who survive it (16-19).

Verses 1-5 are a parallel to the battle-scene described in 12.1-9: the last great siege of Jerusalem. After human defeat (2a), the Lord will intervene with supernatural acts until the moment when He comes for His final victory (5b). The earthquake is that referred to in Amos 1.1, though the escape from Jerusalem is reminiscent of Zedekiah's flight in 587 B.C. (2 Kings 25.4).

Then will come the ending of winter and night, and it will be an era of continuous daylight. As the mountains are turned into a plain, so the city of Jerusalem, rebuilt as in ancient times (Jer. 31.38), will be all the more visibly exalted above it. Geba, ten miles north of Jerusalem, and Rimmon, ten miles north of Beersheba, were the approximate limits of Judah before the exile (2 Kings 23.8). 'Over all the earth' (not just over this land) the Lord will be King, and all men will acknowledge the basic creed of Jewish monotheism (9). These will be the survivors of God's judgements and they will be expected, under threat of drought, to worship annually at Jerusalem at the Feast of Tabernacles, the celebration of the Lord's enthronement as King of the universe. Special sanctions are threatened against Egypt because lack of rain would be no loss to them (18 f.)!

Finally, the prophet's concern for Temple ritual is reflected in vs. 20 f.: sacrifice in abundance is envisaged (cooking pots the size of huge cauldrons, 20b); there will be no need of special utensils, for everything will be sacred to the Lord for all to use (21a); no one will need to trade in the Temple, i.e. to exchange secular for sacred goods (cf. Matt. **21.**12). In the great day that is coming, everything will be sacred to the Lord—right down to the bells on the harness of the horses! Thus is expressed in priestly terms the acme of perfection which is to be found in the new Jerusalem.

Questions for further study and discussion on Zechariah chs. 9–14
1. Study the way in which Jesus fulfilled the prophecy of Zech. **9.**9 (cf. Matt. **21.**1–11; John **12.**12–19). What other predictions in this chapter can He be said to have fulfilled?
2. What is the meaning of the phrase 'the blood of My covenant' (**9.**11)?
3. What light is thrown by these chapters on the meaning of Christ's death?
4. How is the Lord's Kingship described in ch. **14,** in relation to (*a*) the nations, and (*b*) His own people?

Malachi

INTRODUCTION

Whether Malachi (lit. 'my messenger') was the author's name or a *nom de plume* based on 3.1, the book he wrote has a consistency and pattern which assures its unity. Its background is of lax Temple worship (**1.7**), failure to pay tithes (**3.8**), frequent marriage with foreign women (**2.11**): all this at a time when a Persian governor was ruling Judah (**1.8**). Our knowledge of conditions during the Persian period is very limited, but as these were among the evils that Nehemiah tried to rectify (Neh. **13.10, 23 f.**), most commentators date Malachi either just before Nehemiah's governorship (i.e. about 450 B.C.) or in the interval between his first and second periods of administration (i.e. between 444 and 433 B.C.). The message of Malachi may be summed up in the phrase in **1.6**: 'If I am your Master, where is the honour due to Me?'

Malachi 1 — Injured Innocence

A recurring pattern is seen throughout *Malachi* consisting of an accusation by the prophet, followed by a reply of injured innocence ('How have we . . . ?'), which in turn is followed by a more explicit statement of the fault with which the people are charged. This pattern is found in **1.2,6,7; 2.17; 3.7,8,13**.

In this chapter it begins not with an accusation but with the announcement of the Lord's love for Israel. When taxed for evidence of this, the prophet points to the fate of Edom, the nation who had earned such hatred by their betrayal of Jerusalem in 587 B.C., and whose history went back to the rejection of Esau and the choice of Jacob as the heir of the promises to Abraham (Gen. **25.23**). 'Love' clearly means election-love, and 'hate' is its opposite (not an immoral hatred so much as rejection from the position of honour).

If Israel has been chosen to the covenantal father–son relationship with God, he is charged with failing to show his 'senior partner' due respect. The charge is levelled first at the priesthood for their slovenly ways in the Temple. They take the view that anything will do for God, an attitude not peculiar to their day. God could wish that one of the priests saw the hypocrisy of it and had the courage to close down Temple services altogether (10). In comparison with this so-called worship, God was getting better and purer offerings at heathen sanctuaries from Gentile congregations (11). This is a far better interpretation of a difficult verse than to attribute universalism to Malachi or the popular contemporary notion that 'everybody worships the same God under different names'. Such an idea would have been abhorrent to any O.T. writer, and Malachi plays on the incredibility of his statement to shock his readers, or hearers, into seeing the utter unworthiness of their worship.

Verse 13 caricatures the professionalism of the priest who finds his routine duties tedious, and v. 14 castigates the layman who gives God the second best when he has promised Him the best. It is a case of 'like priest, like people': the fault in both cases is that they have lost sight of the greatness of the King, the Lord of hosts (14).

Thought: Only the best is good enough for God.

Malachi 2.1-9   Irresponsible Clergy

The accusation made in 1.6 receives now its condemnation. The duty of the priesthood is made clear: it consists of (*i*) giving true instruction (Heb. *torah*), a word meaning oral direction on matters of ritual, moral and spiritual importance, given in response to an inquiry (6a); (*ii*) unimpeachable conduct, which combines qualities of moral rectitude (righteousness), good relations with others (peace), and awareness of the presence of God (walking with Him); (*iii*) influencing the lives of others positively for good, inducing repentance and true conversion (6b). As he does all this, the priest is fulfilling his intended role as God's messenger and the guardian of God's truth (7). 'Knowledge' (7) is not academic learning, but personal experience of the living God: books are no substitute for this kind of wisdom, though they can, and do, enhance it.

God's expectations of the priesthood are expressed in the phrase, 'My covenant with Levi' (4,8), the patriarch standing for the whole priestly family descended from him. This was intended to be a means of bringing life (= 'blessing'; what the N.T. calls 'abundant life') and peace (social, religious and inner harmony). As with the covenant with Moses on Sinai, it had its sanctions in the form of blessings and curses. The priests, having themselves departed from the requirements of God, were misleading others and thus failing in their duties (8). There was therefore nothing for it but that God should turn the blessings into curses, desecrate the priestly order and remove them from His presence (2 f.).

The passage highlights the crucial influence, for good as well as for harm, that the clergy can exercise through their office; and this applies to the lay preacher who is invested with ministerial responsibilities as well as the ordained clergyman. If their ministry is grounded in the fear of God (5) and their sole concern is to glorify

Him (2), there should be no cause for anxiety. But as soon as they show partiality to those they are called to serve (9), they are on the way to making shipwreck.

Question: Are you fulfilling your responsibilities as a priest (Rev. 5.10)? Could God call you Malachi ('My messenger'; cf. v. 7)?

Malachi 2.10-16   Marriage and Divorce

Quite apart from the failure of the priesthood, Malachi felt that the troubles his people were going through could be attributed to a number of particular points in which they were all falling short. These were (*a*) the general disregard for the sanctity of marriage (2.10–16); (*b*) the carelessness about maintaining the ministry through regular tithing (3.8–12); and (*c*) the general attitude of contempt for God of which these were symptomatic (2.17; 3.13–15).

The question of marriage and divorce he relates to the ineffectiveness of their public worship (13). A man's prayers, as well as his preaching, can all too easily be vitiated by the inconsistency of his marriage relationship. Two evils were prevalent in Malachi's time. The first was contracting marriages with foreign women, whom he describes as daughters of a foreign god (11). To do this was to deny the covenant of Sinai and the Jewish doctrine of election (10). Jews were God's own people, His creation, His offspring (unless we take the 'one father' of v. 10 to be referring to Abraham or Jacob; cf. 3.6). In any event v. 10 means the integral unity of the children of Abraham: it does not teach the 'universal fatherhood of God and brotherhood of man'. That concept is flatly contradicted by what follows. Malachi was in fact saying exactly what Paul was to enlarge upon in 2 Cor. 6.14–18. A chosen people must marry within the community.

The second evil was that of divorcing Jewish wives in order to make these liaisons with foreigners, thus adding to the guilt of the enterprise. The phrase, 'the wife of your youth' (14,15), suggests that it was as the husbands grew older that they put aside their maturing wives in favour of younger and more shapely foreign girls. This practice is attacked on three counts: (*a*) it is a sin against God, for He was the unseen witness to the original marriage covenant (14); (*b*) it frustrates the purpose of God, which is that children are brought up to serve Him in the community of faith (15); and (*c*) it is abhorrent to God because it constitutes cruelty against the rejected wife (16); 'covering one's garment with violence' being a figurative expression for treating one's wife with cruelty.

Note the repetition of 'faithfulness': God expects us to be faithful to our partners, both in marriage and in the faith, and supremely to Himself.

Malachi 2.17-3.5   The God of Justice

The days after the exile saw an age of increasing rationalism. As new patterns were being built up, old values were being questioned and often rejected. Many were sceptical of the old prophetic faith in a righteous God who rewarded the good and punished the wicked. The inequalities of life did not seem to fit into this tidy pattern and so God's justice was frequently called in question. This was no new revolt against the beliefs of past generations: Israel had always had her questioners. But the upheaval of the exile had brought it to the surface and scepticism was on the increase. By Malachi's time even God was tired of it (2.17)! His message was that God was going to act to remedy the injustices of which men were complaining.

3.1 brings together the persons of the forerunner ('My Messenger' = Malachi) and of the Lord who comes to purify the Temple and the priesthood. It seems best to understand 'the messenger of the covenant' as belatedly in apposition to the forerunner, and to take vs. 2 f. as being the activity of the Lord Himself. This does not leave much for the messenger to do, but possibly that was the writer's intention. The forerunner's task is simply to prepare the way and to call attention to the great One who is following behind. He is described in 4.5 as Elijah restored to life again and, of course, in the N.T. as John Baptist.

When the Lord comes, He will (*a*) purify the priesthood so that the worship of Israel may be acceptable (Jesus' action in cleansing the Temple was only a symbolic fulfilment of this and cannot be said to have exhausted its meaning); and (*b*) He will then, and only then, take punitive action against individuals for their acts of injustice (5). The sins mentioned are a combination of infringements of the Ten Commandments and the inhumanities against which the eighth-century prophets preached. The only 'religious' sin is that of sorcery: all the others are anti-social, but in committing them men do in fact show their disrespect for God ('do not fear Me', 5).

Malachi 3.6-18   Giving to God

The first verse of this section presents a problem of interpretation. As it stands in the RSV it means that only God's unchanging mercy prevents the people from being punished with destruction. This is true enough, but it is strange to find a word of mercy following hard on the heels of God's justice (5) and immediately preceding a statement of Israel's persistent disobedience (7). There is something to be said therefore for translating v. 6: 'I the Lord do not change; and you do not cease to be sons of Jacob', i.e. you are inveterate deceivers like your forefather.

When challenged to be specific in His call for repentance, the Lord refers to the issue of paying tithes. A man's money is often a barometer of his whole outlook on life. His treasure goes where his heart goes (Matt. 6.21). No protestation of piety carries weight when it is contradicted by a failure to give sacrificially.

Tithing was a duty more than an option. It involved handing over a tenth of one's produce or income to God as a token of recognition that all increase came from Him and belonged to Him. To pay tithes was not an act of generosity: it was an act of self-deprivation. To the Israelite, giving only began when tithes had been paid. The tithe was a kind of ecclesiastical income-tax, which went to the maintenance of the Temple and its staff; giving was done additionally through hospitality, aid to the poor and the 'free will offering', which was usually given through Temple funds for a special need. It is impossible to apply the same pattern rigorously to present-day Christian needs, but there are obviously basic principles which should be related to our giving, as Christians, to God's work and the needs of others.

The nation's failure to tithe produced the results found in Neh. 13.10–13: Nehemiah the administrator appears to have been more successful than Malachi the preacher! However, despite their withholding of God's dues and their serious questioning of the value of religion (13–15), there was a nucleus of faithful men who had a regard for God and whom He would remember and acknowledge (16 f.).

'Take my silver and my gold,
Not a mite would I withhold. . . .'
True or false?

Malachi 4 — The Day of the Lord

In the final analysis the only answer to the perennial question of the inequality of life, and especially to the complaint expressed in 3.14 f., has to be left to the day of judgement. This is described by Malachi in terms of a consuming fire which will annihilate the wicked as quickly and easily as a farmer burns off a field of stubble when he has harvested the corn. The righteous, on the other hand, will enjoy the sunshine of God's blessing and will rejoice with all the exuberance of calves which have been set free from their stalls to go prancing over the now-blackened stubble-fields (3). The figure of the sun of righteousness with healing in its wings (2) is probably derived from Egyptian or Persian art, which often represents the Sun-god as a winged disc, affording protection and blessing to those who worship it. Malachi saw no harm in borrowing the imagery without taking over the theology that went with it.

Verses 4–6 consist of two postscripts, which could be regarded as rounding off the minor prophets, the Hebrew 'Book of the Twelve', or even as suitable finales to the whole O.T. The first looks back to the beginning of the story: Moses, the covenant, and the commandments (4). The second looks forward to the beginning of a new era: Elijah, heralding the coming of the Messianic age and preparing men's hearts for it. One represents the law and its demands; the other stands for prophecy and its promises. Here were the two main strands of O.T. teaching, sometimes mutually critical but never mutually incompatible. In the years which separated Malachi from the birth of Christ, Judaism developed in different directions. In the religion of the rabbis and the scribes the Law was paramount; but there were other sections of Judaism where the spirit of prophecy was never forgotten (as evidenced by the Qumran community's writings). The period between the Testaments spoke with many conflicting voices, but when Jesus came it was with Moses and Elijah that He appeared on the Mount of Transfiguration, and with whom He discussed the details of His Messiahship. In Him, therefore, as both Prophet and Priest, the two elements of Judaism find their perfect unity.

Questions for further study and discussion on Malachi
1. What may be learnt from **1.6—2.9** about the Christian minister's chief areas of temptation?
2. Is divorce always contrary to the will of God? Cf. **2.16**; and see also Deut. **24.1**; Matt. **5.31** f.; **19.3–9**; Luke **16.18**; 1 Cor. **7.10–16**.
3. What principles of Christian giving may be deduced from **3.8–12**?
4. In what way does the book of *Malachi* prepare the reader for the N.T. dispensation?